Every last Crumb

Every last Crumb

From fresh loaf to final crust,
recipes to make
the most of your bread

James Ramsden

PAVILION

Pavilion
An imprint of HarperCollinsPublishers Ltd
1 London Bridge Street
London SE1 9GF

www.harpercollins.co.uk

HarperCollinsPublishers
1st Floor, Watermarque Building
Ringsend Road Dublin 4
Ireland

10 9 8 7 6 5 4 3 2 1

First published in Great Britain by
Pavilion, an imprint of HarperCollinsPublishers Ltd 2022

ISBN 978-1-911663-99-7

This book is produced from independently certified FSC™ paper
to ensure responsible forest management.

For more information visit:
www.harpercollins.co.uk/green

Reproduction by Mission Productions, Hong Kong
Printed and bound in China by Toppan Leefung Ltd

Commissioning Editor: Cara Armstrong
Copy Editor: Stephanie Evans
Design Manager: Nicky Collings
Layout Designer: Lizzie Ballantyne
Illustrator: Ellie Edwards

WHEN USING KITCHEN APPLIANCES PLEASE ALWAYS FOLLOW THE
MANUFACTURER'S INSTRUCTIONS

CONTENTS

Introduction

This isn't so much a book about baking as it is one about cooking and, above all, a book about eating.

Because, lovely as baking is, I'm far more interested in what comes next; in the life of the loaf. Congratulations, you have baked – or bought – some bread: now what are you going to do with it?

Much like the rest of the country – or so it seemed – 2020's first nationwide lockdown rekindled a hitherto dormant interest in making bread in our house. Where previously we'd knocked out the odd loaf perhaps once every few months, now we were baking every other day or two. There were mornings when I'd set my alarm for silly o'clock so that the dough I'd been proving overnight could be baked and cooled in time for breakfast. We started discussing the behaviour and misbehaviour of our starter, levain and dough as if they were additional and even more time-consuming children than the two cabin-fevered lunatics we already shared a home with. There were arguments over whose turn it was to feed the starter.

If this all sounds like a mad hassle then you are in luck – you don't have to do any of that to enjoy this book. You just need access to half-decent bread (though plenty of these recipes will sing well enough with sliced white), and an appetite for gluten. If baking is something you'd like to explore, there are people far more qualified than I am to guide you through the occasionally torturous process of producing a good loaf of bread.

So, whether you're at the hydration-percentage-chatting, baking-obsessed end of the spectrum or are far happier mooching down to the shop to buy a loaf, here is a basketful of recipes to help you make the most of your bread.

HOW STALE IS YOUR BREAD?

The book is divided into chapters that arrange themselves roughly around how a loaf of bread develops and, inevitably, deteriorates, over the course of five days. This is far from set in stone. Loaves behave differently depending on a range of factors: the amount of salt they contain, the humidity of the kitchen, where – and how – they're stored, the hydration of the loaf, and whether or not Mercury is in retrograde. All of these things (except perhaps the last!) will have a significant effect on how stale your loaf is on day two, day three, day five. So, consider the organization of the chapters to be a very loose guide and do bear in mind that if you're absolutely jonesing to make the meatloaf in Chapter 5 but only have a Chapter 2 loaf ... it will be fine.

SOURDOUGH IS NOT THE ONLY BREAD

But which bread? It's quite a broad church and I'm more than wary of marauding into multiple culinary and cultural heffalump traps. This book is predominantly eurocentric and ultimately sourdough-ish in its attack. That is not because I'm uninterested in other breads; I have dived head-first into my fair share of roti, mopped many acres of sauced plates with naan, fizzily chewed on sour injera, torn hunks of challah, and picked at paratha with as much love and glee as any bread – that's the point of bread, isn't it? But unlike when it comes to eating bread, with recipe-writing I know my limits. And, as with baking, I am fully aware that there are many people more qualified than I am to expand on the big, beautiful world of bread.

So this is my small, domestic bread world, one that largely revolves around the handful of loaves I grew up with, and more specifically around the sourdough loaf that appears in our house every few days, whether by my own hand or someone else's. Sometimes I will offer a few suggestions for which breads might be appropriate but as with most things I say, consider these to be guidelines, not gospel.

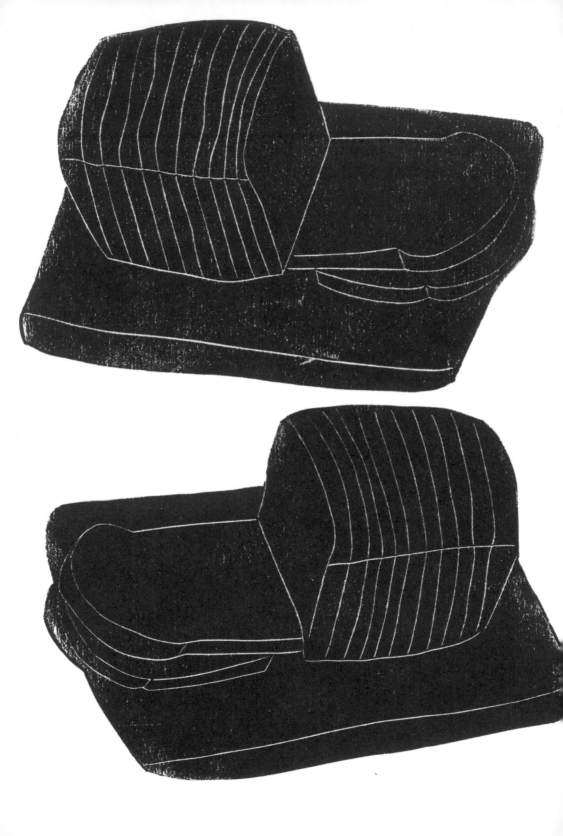

DAY ONE

A Fresh loaf

There is fresh bread and there is fresh bread. In this chapter
I'm talking about bread so fresh – a minimum of 2, a maximum of
12 hours out of the oven – that slicing it any less than an inch thick
requires concentration and a very good knife; bread that feels so light
that it might float off at any moment; bread that smells deeply of wheat and
yeast and savouriness, with a crust that crackles and sings under pressure;
bread that, when compressed by a careless hand or in an overstuffed
bread bin, will struggle to return to its original shape.

Herein lies all the potential that follows in this book. While I'm not saying
that this newborn bread is inherently better than its increasingly
ageing self, it is bread at its most essential. It is, I would argue – if not
insist – the only stage at which bread is satisfying without any addition,
augmentation or alteration.

If, therefore, this chapter feels a little light in terms of the number of
recipes, that's because, on the whole, the freshest loaf needs the least
doing to it. There is of course an endless number of sandwiches you can
make, but that would just turn this into a sandwich book. Which it is not –
although there are a few sandwiches here. I like sandwiches.

Bread with butter and jam

If this doesn't read like a half-hearted recipe title then I don't know what does (potentially the one in a book I once owned that suggests in the desserts section a bar of chocolate), but I would like your permission to express my love for this admittedly Blyton-ish combination.

On those mornings when I have the energy to slope down to the kitchen at 5am to bake bread in time for breakfast, this is what I have. In fact, it's the reason I get up so early, giving the bread time to cool (just) before we eat. Toasting bread this fresh would be a terrible solecism. Just eat in thick slices, with excessive amounts of butter and great spoonfuls of jam or honey.

I could leave it there, but because you have bought this book – or even if you've stolen it, or are perhaps reading it over someone's shoulder on the bus – I'll treat you to a recipe for homemade butter (couldn't be easier) and a nice jam recipe (likewise).

One sourdough, bloomer, baguette – baked or bought within the last 8 hours, ideally only just cooled from the oven.

For the butter
600ml/20fl oz good quality double/heavy cream
Sea salt, a pinch (optional but recommended)

For the jam
500g/1lb 2oz blueberries (fresh, or thawed if frozen)
    makes 1 large jar
300g/10½oz granulated sugar
2 tbsp lemon juice, fresh or from a bottle
A bay leaf or a vanilla pod, if you like – though unadulterated
    is fine by me

Making butter is much like doing yoga, in that it sounds like a hassle, and can be painful, but you're always glad you've done it. And it's better than yoga, in that you get to eat butter afterwards.

Put the cream in a stand mixer with a paddle (correct equipment) or in a large jar (painful but worth it) and mix on a fairly high setting, or shake vigorously if using a jar. Keep going. It will become softly whipped cream, and then stiff cream, and then it will split. Keep going still. Add the salt at this point, if using. Keep going. Eventually you will have a solid mass of butter, and a delicious puddle of buttermilk for making pancakes or soda bread or fried chicken.

With clean hands, squeeze the butter tenderly to rid it of any excess buttermilk, then shape into a log. Wrap in baking paper/parchment. Refrigerate if not applying to bread immediately. It will keep for a couple of weeks in the fridge.

For your jam, stick a plate in the freezer. Tip the blueberries into a saucepan along with the sugar, lemon juice and bay leaf/vanilla pod if using. Stir over a medium-high heat, lightly squashing the fruit as you do, until the sugar has dissolved, and the pan is beginning to simmer. Reduce the temperature and simmer for 25–30 minutes without covering, stirring occasionally, until jammy. Put a small dollop on your now-frozen plate and pop it in the fridge for a few minutes. Now nudge it with a clean finger – if the jam wrinkles, it's ready. If not, simmer for another 5 minutes and repeat the test, until it does. Cool, and store in a sterilized jar.

Five sandwiches for fresh bread

Part – though certainly not all – of the reason for toasting (lightly, lightly) your bread before its sandwichification is to provide structural integrity. But the freshest loaf is best, in my humble submission, rendered into a sandwich without passing through a toaster. This can cause problems with disintegration if you don't select your fillings with great care, or slice your bread with sufficient girth. Or, ultimately, eat the thing with reasonable urgency.

Here are four sandwiches that are best made with fresh, untoasted bread.

A CHEESE SANDWICH OF THE NOT-GRILLED VARIETY

I kind of liked the idea of doing an amped-up version of the (relatively) old classic brie and cranberry and this was the result. It's kitsch and surprisingly rewarding. Baron Bigod is a spectacularly good brie-style cheese from Suffolk; if you can't get it, then brie is fine.

The quantities here make more dressing and pickled grapes than you'll need but I'm sure they'll find their uses – and they keep well.

MAKES 1 SANDWICH

For the dressing
100ml/3½fl oz cranberry juice
1 tbsp red wine vinegar
1 garlic clove, lightly crushed
100ml/3½fl oz olive oil
1 tsp honey

For the pickled grapes
100ml/3½fl oz white wine vinegar
50g/1¾oz caster/superfine sugar
Pinch of salt
200g/7oz black grapes, halved and pitted

For the rest
2 slices of fresh bread, or a small baguette, split lengthways
75–100g/2¾–3½oz ripe Baron Bigod cheese or brie, sliced
A good handful of watercress
A few walnuts, chopped and lightly toasted

Put the cranberry juice, red wine vinegar and garlic in a small pan, bring to the boil, and reduce by about two-thirds. Discard the garlic, cool, then whisk in the olive oil and honey.

For the grapes, whisk the white wine vinegar, sugar and pinch of salt in a large bowl until the sugar has dissolved. Add the grapes, stir and leave to pickle for at least 2 hours.

Take your bread and arrange the cheese within. Top with pickled grapes and watercress. Dress the leaves with the cranberry vinaigrette. Finish with a few chopped walnuts and eat.

GRILLED MACKEREL WITH HORSERADISH CRÈME FRAÎCHE, DILL, ROCKET AND CAPERS

Dill was one of those herbs I couldn't quite get my head around until I spent a few months in Russia. The locals seemed to festoon most things with it and slowly I became accustomed to its peculiar flavour. Needless to say, if in the great game of dill or no dill you shoot for no dill, then drop it, or sub it out for parsley, fennel or, should you have access, horseradish shoots.

If you're one of those 'food needs crunch' people, you can pop in some Gem lettuce, but I quite enjoy the pillowy softness of this one.

MAKES 1 SANDWICH

1 tbsp freshly grated horseradish or strong horseradish sauce
4 tsp crème fraîche
½ small garlic clove, crushed
A squeeze of lemon juice
1–2 mackerel fillets, unskinned (about 125g/4½oz in total)
1 tbsp plain/all-purpose flour
20g/¾oz unsalted butter
2 slices of fresh white bread (or granary, bap, flatbread)
A handful of picked dill fronds
A good handful of rocket/arugula leaves
1 tsp capers
1 tsp finely chopped shallot
Fine sea salt and freshly ground black pepper

Combine the horseradish, crème fraîche and garlic and add a squeeze of lemon juice to taste. Set aside.

Dust the mackerel in the flour and ½ teaspoon of fine sea salt and pat off any excess. Drop the butter into a hot non-stick frying pan or skillet and let it skid around for a few seconds and melt. When bubbling gently, carefully lower in the mackerel, skin-side down, and gently sit a flat pan lid on top to prevent excess curling. Cook for 3 minutes on the skin side. Turn and cook for a further minute or so, until cooked through. Set aside.

Spread your bread with the horseradish crème fraîche. Add the mackerel, dill, rocket, capers and shallot. Finish with a comical amount of black pepper.

A CHICKEN SANDWICH

I'm not sharing the chicken sandwich recipe we serve at my sandwich shop in King's Cross, Sons + Daughters, because my business partner Sam would kill me. This one is just as delicious. You'll have to roast a chicken first – use the juices and leftover chicken from the recipe on page 90 (without the bread trivet), or whatever roast chicken you have lying around on a Monday.

Dealer's choice as far as the bread goes – I'd choose bloomer, sourdough, baguette or focaccia.

MAKES 1 SANDWICH

2 tbsp mayonnaise
1 roast garlic clove, mashed
1 tbsp roasting juices from the tin
1 tsp Dijon mustard
½ lemon
2 slices of bread
125g/4½oz roast chicken
A few Gem lettuce leaves
A few anchovy fillets (optional of course)
Watercress
Salt and freshly ground black pepper, if necessary

Combine the mayonnaise, garlic, roasting juices and mustard with a gentle squeeze of lemon – just enough to give it some zing, as opposed to creating anything obviously 'lemony' (what a word).

Spread the top and bottom slices of bread with the mayonnaise. Build the sandwich with the remaining ingredients. Add a few twists of pepper. Salt may be necessary if you are omitting the anchovies and/or using under-seasoned roast chicken.

Should you find yourself tempted to add further condiments – Parmesan, sriracha, pesto, mango chutney etc – then do. More is more.

PORK AND EGG BANJO

An egg banjo is so named because of the action performed – one hand removing the sandwich from harm's way, the other frantically wiping your jumper clean – when your first mouthful leads to the inevitable fugitive egg yolk down your front. The full George Formby.

This was inspired by the katsu sando – a Japanese drinking snack – which was all the rage for a time in London's restaurants, partly because they look good on Instagram, but more importantly because they are delicious. This version is breakfast-appropriate but don't let that stop you eating it any time of day.

MAKES 1 SANDWICH

For the sauce
2 tbsp ketchup
A few shakes of Worcestershire sauce
1 enthusiastic tsp English mustard
½ tsp runny honey

For the pork
100g/3½oz pork loin, skinless and boneless
1 tbsp plain/all-purpose flour, seasoned with salt
1 egg, beaten
50g/1¾oz breadcrumbs (panko would be the go-to but in the spirit
    of this book, whatever breadcrumbs you have to hand)

For the rest
4 tbsp groundnut/peanut or other neutral oil
1 egg
2 slices of soft white bread
25g/1oz shredded white cabbage
Squeezy mayonnaise – Kewpie if you can find it

Make the sauce by combining the ingredients. Take a well-earned rest.

Ready to continue? Lightly beat the pork to flatten it into a piece of even thickness. Bonus points if you can make it roughly the same dimensions as your bread.

Dust the pork in the flour, turn it in the beaten egg and coat thoroughly in the breadcrumbs.

Get the groundnut oil hot in a non-stick pan over a medium-high heat and add the breaded pork. Fry for 3 minutes or so on each side until golden and crisp. Remove and rest. Add the egg and fry. While that's frying, spread the bread top and bottom with the sauce. Add the pork, then your fried egg and then the cabbage. Dress the cabbage with mayonnaise and complete the sandwich building.

Eat.

FRITTO MISTO SANDWICH

As with the Pork and Egg Banjo (page 16), this sandwich combines days one and five of the chapters in this book, requiring as it does both fresh bread and breadcrumbs. The two recipes are also semi-subliminal tributes to one of our favourite restaurants in London.

Credit for this idea really goes to food writer (and friend) George Reynolds, who suggested we do it at the sandwich shop. We hadn't got round to figuring it out when Bright, beloved London Fields restaurant in neighbouring Hackney, got in there first. Bastards. They do fried squid in a brioche bun and it slaps, as the cool kids say.

Anyway, here's my 'take'. It's tempting to stick some lettuce or even thinly sliced and dressed fennel in there, but I quite like the pared-backness of this.

If you're wondering why this serves two when the other sandwiches serve one, I have no good answer for that, other than the fact the fishmonger looked like he wanted to throw me through the window when I asked for 50g/1¾oz monkfish.

MAKES 2 SANDWICHES

100g/3½oz cleaned squid, rings and tentacles
100g/ 3½oz monkfish, cubed
6 raw prawns, de-shelled and de-veined
3 tbsp seasoned plain/all-purpose flour
2 eggs, beaten with a splash of milk
100g/3½oz fine dried breadcrumbs
750ml/25fl oz groundnut/peanut or other neutral oil
4 tbsp mayonnaise
½ garlic clove, crushed
1 tbsp sriracha
4 slices of fresh white bread – bloomer, ideally; some focaccia
    or 2 brioche buns would also work
½ lemon
1 tbsp finely chopped parsley
A pinch of chilli flakes

Toss the squid, monkfish and prawns in the seasoned flour, then coat in the egg wash, and finally roll in the breadcrumbs.

Heat the oil in a large pan or wok to 170°C/340°F, or until a cube of bread fizzles and turns golden within 30 seconds.

Fry the fish for 2–3 minutes until crisp and golden. Remove with a slotted spoon and drain on kitchen paper. Mix the mayonnaise, garlic and sriracha and spread on your bread. Add the fried fish, give it a good sprinkling of lemon juice, parsley and chilli flakes. Eat.

Anchoïade and crudités

If you are not an anchovy fiend, you may want to turn the page now: this is not the recipe to convert you. Perhaps that is pathetically defeatist (and if you think it is then please by all means dive in) but the anchovy punch delivered here is gloriously unapologetic. That it is bolstered by a not-ungenerous amount of raw garlic is either the icing on the cake or the nail in the coffin, depending on your palate.

Fresh baguette – or if you want to be uber-echt, fougasse – would be the way forward for me here, though no one is going to complain if you're serving focaccia, ciabatta or straight-up sourdough.

And actually you could nudge this into the next chapter and serve with toast – to wit, there's an enhanced version, *anchoïade à la dracenoise* (not, alas, 'dragon-style', but in the style of Draguignan, although it amounts to the same thing, etymologically at least, in the south of France) – mix with onions and chopped hard-boiled eggs, spread thickly on toast and pop under the grill/broiler. Probably not one for a first date.

This particular version comes via a nineteenth-century French gastronome and polymath, Austin de Croze. The orange-flower water seems like a genuinely unhinged piece of improvisation but produces something ethereally good that can double up as a sauce for grilled lamb. I'll shut up now.

For the anchoïade
24 anchovy fillets
12 blanched almonds
3 dried figs, roughly chopped
2 garlic cloves, roughly chopped
Pinch of chilli flakes
4 tbsp fruity olive oil
1 shallot, chopped
1 tbsp each of chopped parsley, chives, tarragon, fennel and basil
Juice of ½ lemon
½ tsp orange-flower water

For scooping
Thickly sliced fresh bread
Raw vegetables arranged as artfully as you can be bothered,
    for preference:
    – Breakfast radishes, leaves left intact
    – Candy beetroot, cut into wedges
    – Chicory, leaves separated
    – Mangetouts/snow peas
    – Cucumber, wedged
    – Kohlrabi, cut into chunks
    – Celery, sticks trimmed and separated

Pop all the ingredients for the anchoïade in a blender and blend until smooth, adding a little water to loosen if necessary. Serve with the bread and crudités.

Dukkah and olive oil

Here's a surprising little treat to drop onto the coffee table or kitchen island or wherever you put things to chew on that aren't necessarily dinner. Dukkah is a spice and seed mix that is popular in Egypt and the Middle East. You tear a hunk of bread then you dunk it in the olive oil and then into the dukkah and then into your mouth. And of course you don't double dip anymore, but then I'm sure you never did.

MAKES 1 JAR OF DUKKAH

4 tbsp blanched hazelnuts
2 tbsp white sesame seeds
2 tbsp coriander seeds
1 tbsp cumin seeds
1 tbsp nigella seeds
1 tbsp marjoram leaves, roughly torn (optional*)
½ tsp sea salt

To serve
Fresh sourdough
Olive oil

Put a dry frying pan or skillet over a medium heat and, in separate batches, toast the hazelnuts, sesame, coriander, cumin and nigella seeds until fragrant. Cool completely, then pound in a pestle and mortar until loose and granular – you're not looking for a powder. Stir through the marjoram and salt and check for seasoning. This dukkah will be excellent in a jar for at least a week and will keep much longer, though it loses its oomph after a time. Serve with the bread and olive oil.

*I do find the addition of the word 'optional' to ingredients lists unhelpful, because it suggests the other ingredients are compulsory, whereas most of the time they're not, but I've said the marjoram is optional because, for reasons I can't understand, this herb can be hard to come by. You can always substitute oregano, which is a slightly more punchy, less elegant cousin.

Roasted cherry tomatoes with goat's curd and herbs

Part of me feels that tomatoes are like clams – sure, they are delicious in and of themselves, but more delicious, almost always, is the juice that seeps out when you cook them. A cherry tomato is a lovely thing. Pop it in your mouth and have yourself a wild time. Roast it, on the other hand, with an Oliverian amount of olive oil with salt and herbs, and the intensity of flavour that you'll find in the cooking juices is as beautiful and rewarding as any consommé you've spent five hours making.

Serve this as a simple starter or even a cheese course.

SERVES 4

750g/1lb 10oz cherry tomatoes
5 tbsp olive oil
A few sprigs of fresh thyme
A few sprigs of rosemary
1–2 tbsp white balsamic vinegar (or cider, or white wine vinegar),
    depending on the natural acidity of the tomatoes
150g/5½oz goat's curd, or soft goat's cheese or, at a push, mozzarella
A few basil leaves, roughly torn
Fresh bread
Flaky sea salt and freshly ground black pepper

Preheat the oven to 200°C fan/220°C/425°F/gas mark 7. Tip the tomatoes into a roasting tin with the oil, herbs, a good pinch of flaky salt and a twist of black pepper and toss everything to coat. Roast for 20–25 minutes until the tomatoes are blistered and juicy. Leave to cool, then lightly press to encourage the juice of the tomatoes to give a little more of itself. Taste and add a little white balsamic vinegar, if it needs a further pop of acidity.

Serve the tomatoes with the goat's curd and a few torn basil leaves and some fresh bread for scooping and mopping. The tomatoes will keep for five days in a jar in the fridge.

DAY TWO

Toast & Friends

'My hour for tea is half-past five, and my buttered toast waits for nobody.'
Wilkie Collins, *The Woman in White*

'Brown for first course, white for pudding. Brown's savoury, white's the treat.
Of course, I'm the one who's laughing because I actually love brown toast.'
Mark Corrigan, *Peep Show*

It's after your loaf has had a day or so to have a good think about life
that you might start pondering toast. And what a thing to ponder.
I become a little single-minded when there is toast about – or, rather, bread
for toasting. Having prepared the coffee or tea, I will slice
the bread and pop it in the toaster, arranging, as it toasts, what I like
to think of as The Toast Station, viz: a breakfast plate, a knife, a butter knife,
a teaspoon or two (to prevent any cross-contamination between crumbs,
butter and spreads) and then of course butter and honey, jam,
Marmite or marmalade, or if it's a very special day, all of the above.
I'm never sure if my wife finds the whole thing bizarre, hilarious or
tiresome. It's possibly all three. Either way, whatever carnage is going on
around me, this will be my focus and I'll sit down ready to lean into a
serious toast session. At this point, inevitably, the children will decide they
quite fancy some toast too, and my four slices quickly become two and this
little paradise I've spent 10 minutes creating is very much lost.

The upside is that I still get to eat some toast, and as you may have gathered
from this account, I do love toast.

Pan con tomate

This is no more my recipe than I could claim a ragu or a curry or a quiche or a steak was my recipe. It's just a recipe. It's probably time food writers stopped feeling obliged to add a 'twist' or a 'take' to classics and staples; we should just relate how we go about these things and give credit to those who – implicitly or explicitly – inspired, taught, lived, breathed these dishes.

I do enjoy the versions of this Spanish staple at Barrafina, the London-based mini-chain of tapas bars, with its mound of grated tomato pulp on toasted sourdough and its aggressive white peppering, or at Sabor off Regent Street where Nieves Barragán Mohacho festoons the toasts with Iberico ham, but my first memory of being shown the way – vague though it is (the memory, not the method) – was by Catalan cooking expert and Radio 4 panellist Rachel McCormack more than a decade ago. It feels about right.

Use any 'rustic' white bread – sourdough, baguette, etc. Ciabatta works nicely too.

MAKES 4

4 slices of day-old bread
1 garlic clove, halved
2 ripe-to-overripe tomatoes, halved
Good olive oil
Sea salt flakes

Realistically you're not lighting a barbecue to make toast. If you have one lit already, or a good griddle, then crack on with that. Otherwise, just toast the bread. In a toaster.

Rub each slice first with the garlic, then vigorously with half a tomato, smooshing it (technical term) so the juice from the tomato soaks in and the pulp sits on the toast here and there – the bread should be toasted well enough that it provides some grip against the tomato as you smoosh. Give each toast a few generous shakes of olive oil, and finish with a good pinch of sea salt, and pepper if you like (I like), although Rachel told me that Catalans only use pepper in escabeche.

Beef tartare

The Italians have a dandy flavouring technique whereby they rub a wooden board with cut garlic and furiously chop a fistful of rosemary on it before having a go at mincing the beef – it infuses the meat without overpowering it and is quite a subtle trick, as long as you remember to use the garlic and rosemary for another purpose, because the planet is dying and wasting food is bad.

Exacting/uptight French cooks will tell you to use fillet for a tartare but that's almost certainly excessive on the wallet. Rump, bavette and even heart work very well. Make sure your knife is sharper than a serpent's tooth, and your beef is well chilled, both of which will make the chopping operation easier.

SERVES 4 AS A STARTER

1 garlic clove, halved
A few sprigs of rosemary, needles only
250g/9oz beef rump
2 tbsp very finely chopped shallot
1 tbsp very finely chopped capers
1 tbsp finely chopped parsley
1 tbsp ketchup
A few shakes of both Tabasco and Worcestershire sauce
4 slices of bread
4 egg yolks
50g/1¾oz Ossau-Iraty, pecorino or other hard sheep's cheese, grated
Salt and freshly ground black pepper

As explained in the intro, rub your chopping board with the cut garlic clove, then finely chop your rosemary. Put the rosemary to one side and save it for a rainy day (it will freeze).

Slice the beef thinly, then chop. How thoroughly is up to you – some like it rough, some like it fine. Personally I prefer mine at the mincier end of the spectrum. Mix with the shallot, capers, parsley, ketchup, Tabasco and Worcestershire sauce. Taste for seasoning and add a little salt if necessary, which it will be (note also that the egg yolk that follows will take the edge off the seasoning, including the punch of Tabasco, so best to go a little long at this point).

Toast the bread well – it wants to be crunchy. Top the tartare with the egg yolk and cheese and serve with the toast.

Broad beans with burrata, rosemary and garlic

I greatly miss El Parador in Mornington Crescent – a tapas restaurant that closed a few years ago. Camden Town was too far away from me for it ever to become a regular spot, but in the right conditions its garden was the best place to eat in London. They did a little tapa of broad bean and rosemary purée, which inspired this. You could leave out the burrata and serve the beans as a side to grilled lamb or chicken.

SERVES 4

1kg/2lb 4oz young broad beans, podded
100ml/3½fl oz olive oil, plus extra if required
2 garlic cloves, one thinly sliced, one crushed
Needles from a rosemary sprig
4 slices of sourdough
4 burratina, or 2 halved burrata
Salt, to taste, likewise pepper

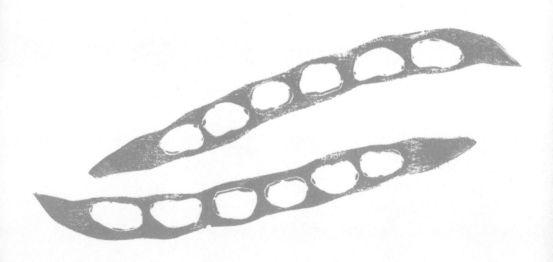

Bring a pan of lightly salted water to the boil and drop in the podded broad beans. Simmer for 2 minutes, drain, and transfer to a deep bowl of iced water. After a couple of minutes drain again. Put on the radio or your favourite podcast and enjoy the mindless repetition of shelling the beans. (Compost the grey shells, or toss in polenta, deep fry and eat as a snack.)

Heat the oil in a large frying pan or skillet over a medium heat and fry the sliced garlic until crisp and golden, then remove with a slotted spoon onto kitchen paper. Add the crushed garlic to the pan along with the rosemary and fry for 30 seconds or so, then add the beans and toss about until warm through. Transfer to a food processor and pulse into a purée, adding a little more oil if needed. Taste for seasoning and adjust with salt if necessary.

Toast the bread, then top with the purée and burrata. Finish with a pinch of salt, the crispy garlic and a drizzle of olive oil.

A bruschetta for each season

Look, you can pronounce it however you like as far as I'm concerned, but just in case you mind about these things as much as some native speakers (and most food snobs) do, it's 'broo-skett-a', not 'broo-shett-a'.

And here's one for each season to get your chops around. If you find yourself wondering why these count as bruschetta while other 'things on toast' in this chapter do not, that would be a fair enough question. For me, there's a sense that to qualify as bruschetta it needs to involve quite a lot of olive oil and garlic, and be relatively minimalist. But we could argue about this all day long. Italians probably do.

SPRING – ASPARAGUS, PECORINO AND PINE NUTS

SERVES 4

1 tbsp pine nuts
500g/1lb 2oz young asparagus, trimmed and cut into
    even-sized pieces
4 slices of sourdough or other rustic loaf
1 garlic clove, halved
Extra virgin olive oil
50g/1¾oz pecorino or Parmesan cheese, finely grated
Mint leaves, roughly torn
½ lemon
Sea salt and freshly ground black pepper

In a dry frying pan or skillet, lightly toast the pine nuts, taking care not to burn them. Leave to cool.

Bring a pot of lightly salted water to the boil and simmer the asparagus for 2 minutes, then drain.

Meanwhile, toast the slices of bread and rub with the garlic. Slosh with a good amount of olive oil, then top with the asparagus, pecorino and mint leaves. Finish with a squeeze of lemon, a generous final slug of olive oil, some sea salt and a twist of black pepper.

SUMMER – CONFIT GARLIC, ARTICHOKE AND FRESH HERBS

It's worth making extra confit garlic here – it's not something you'll ever regret having in the fridge.

SERVES 4

25g/1oz picked herbs and leaves – parsley, chervil, mint, lovage, dill, oregano, nasturtium, baby watercress – at least three of these
4 slices of sourdough or other rustic loaf
1 tbsp white balsamic or cider vinegar
3 tbsp olive oil
A jar of marinated artichokes
1 tbsp very finely chopped chives
Edible flowers, if not inconvenient
Sea salt

For the confit garlic
1 garlic bulb, cloves separated and peeled
100–150ml/3½–5fl oz olive oil

Put the garlic cloves in a small pan and cover with the olive oil. Place over a low heat and gently cook for 30–45 minutes until the garlic is tender – take care not to let the oil go above 90°C/194°F. Remove from the heat, cool and transfer both the garlic and its oil to a sterilized jar.

Pick through your herbs carefully, getting rid of any discoloured leaves or stems, and toss them gently together.

Toast the bread slices. Meanwhile, whisk together the vinegar and the 3 tablespoons of olive oil.

To serve, mash a few garlic cloves into each slice of toast along with a good amount of the oil from the jar. Top with a few marinated artichokes and the herbs. Dress with the vinaigrette and finish with the chopped chives, edible flowers if using, and a good pinch of sea salt.

AUTUMN – FIGS, PROSCIUTTO AND SALTED RICOTTA

If you can't find salted ricotta (*ricotta salata*), pecorino or Parmesan will work here.

SERVES 4

4 fresh figs
1 tbsp balsamic vinegar
2 tbsp olive oil, plus extra for drizzling
4 slices of sourdough or other rustic loaf
1 garlic clove, halved
4 slices of prosciutto
50g/1¾oz ricotta salata
A handful of watercress or rocket/arugula
Sea salt and freshly ground black pepper

Preheat the oven to 180°C fan/200°C/400°F/gas mark 6. Sit the figs in a small roasting tin, cut a cross in the top of each fig, spoon over the balsamic vinegar and olive oil and add a pinch of sea salt. Roast for 12–15 minutes until cooked. Quarter and set aside.

Toast the bread, rub with the garlic and a little olive oil. Top each slice with four pieces of fig and a slice of prosciutto, then shave over the ricotta using a peeler. Garnish with a few salad leaves, then finish with a twist of pepper and a little olive oil.

WINTER – CAVOLO NERO AND BOTTARGA

I first encountered bottarga when living as a student in Paris.* Our neighbour had a house in Sardinia, as one does, and gave us a packet for Christmas. I'm not going to lie, we were a little flummoxed by this sheathed amber putty that tasted for all the world like fishy wax.

Bottarga is salted, cured fish roe from tuna or mullet. Its unique savoury flavour has grown on me since that first encounter, though is probably best enjoyed as part of a dish – say grated over pasta or sliced very thinly onto toasted baguette – not gnawed at like a dehydrated hot dog, which is what the roe pouch looks like.

*Rereading that sentence didn't feel great, if I'm honest – it's the sort of line that would irritate me in someone else's book – but I am honest, and that is where I first encountered it. So.

SERVES 4

200g/7oz cavolo nero, stalks removed, roughly chopped
4 slices of sourdough or other rustic loaf
1 garlic clove, halved
Olive oil
Zest and juice of 1 lemon
A length of bottarga
Sea salt and freshly ground black pepper

Bring a pan of salted water to the boil and add the cavolo nero. Simmer for 2 minutes.

Meanwhile, toast the bread before rubbing it with the garlic and a few flicks of olive oil. Drain the cavolo nero thoroughly and toss through some olive oil and lemon juice to coat, then place on top of the toast. Grate over a generous drift of bottarga, then a little lemon zest. Finish with black pepper and, if necessary, a pinch of sea salt (the bottarga is salty).

Mushrooms on toast

The key here is cooking the onions for the longest time you can bear over the lowest heat you can muster.

SERVES 4

75g/2¾oz butter
2 brown onions, very thinly sliced
2 sprigs of thyme
1 garlic clove, minced
100ml/3½fl oz dry marsala, or other nutty fortified wine
500g/1lb 2oz mushrooms – a mixture of your choosing – roughly chopped
200ml/7fl oz double/heavy cream
A handful of flat-leaf parsley, finely chopped
½ lemon
4 slices of sourdough or other rustic loaf
Salt and freshly ground black pepper

Melt 50g/1¾oz of the butter in a large pan over a low heat and add the onions and thyme. Season with salt, stir to coat, cover and cook for 45 minutes, stirring occasionally, until the onions are melting and golden. Cook, uncovered, for a further 15 minutes until lightly browned.

Add the garlic and cook for a further minute or two. Ratchet up the temperature and add the marsala. Simmer until reduced well into the onions (so that there's no real liquid remaining), then add the mushrooms and stir again. Now add the cream, swirl around a little, then simmer over a medium heat, stirring frequently, until the mushrooms are cooked through, and the liquid they have released has reduced. Check for seasoning and add salt if necessary and pepper if you like pepper. Stir through the parsley and a squeeze of lemon, then keep warm over a gentle heat.

Toast the bread, and butter it with the remaining butter. Top with the mushrooms. Serve.

Cheese toast

I don't think there are many foods that make me as happy as a cheese toastie, or grilled cheese (I think I prefer the American nomenclature to be honest, despite the fact that these aren't, you know, grilled). And yet arguably unlike some other comfort staples – mac and cheese, cottage pie, lasagne, sticky toffee pudding – it can be endlessly adapted without, in my opinion at least, incurring that bathetic moment of: 'It's nice, but not as nice as just a plain cheese toastie.' So here are three cheese toasties that have been enhanced to varying degrees. Remove bells and whistles at will.

CHEESE AND ONION TOASTIE

Somehow it feels that spring onion is the move here – as opposed to brown or white – and I'm not 100% sure why but I think it might be something to do with childhood flashbacks to Morrisons frozen pizza – hot slices of watery tomato, and that not totally lovely flavour raw onion takes on when it's been sliced long ago, kept in a freezer for several months, and then introduced all-too-briefly to an oven.

Anyway, roll with brown, white or red onion if you don't have a spring onion, but maybe sweat it for 15 minutes before you move forward.

SERVES 1

2 slices of bread
15g/½oz softened butter
1 generous tsp Dijon mustard
25g/1oz mature Cheddar cheese, grated
25g/1oz Comté cheese, grated
1 spring onion/scallion, thinly sliced
Freshly ground black pepper
2 tsp mayonnaise

Spread one slice of bread with the butter and mustard, and top the other slice with the cheese and spring onions. Season with black pepper, then put your mustard-butter slice on top of the cheese slice and press down. Spread the outsides, top and bottom, with the mayonnaise.

Pop a cast iron or non-stick frying pan or skillet over a medium heat and get it hot but not too hot – it certainly shouldn't be thinking about smoking. Carefully place the sandwich in the pan and put something heavy-ish and flat on top – a pan lid, for example. Cook for 3–4 minutes until golden and crisp. Turn over and repeat, until the cheese is fully melted. Eat as soon as it is safe to do so.

CHEDDAR, SPICED CHICKPEA AND MANGO CHUTNEY TOASTIE

I'm just going to go right ahead and contradict what I said about onion in the previous recipe. Finely chopped red onion is the move here. Geeta's Mango Chutney for preference, too.

SERVES 1

1 tbsp groundnut/peanut or vegetable oil
65g/2¼oz canned chickpeas, drained, rinsed and dried
½ tsp coriander seeds, very lightly crushed
½ tsp mild curry powder
Pinch of salt
2 tbsp finely chopped red onion
1 tsp finely chopped green chilli
A handful of chopped coriander/cilantro
50g/1¾oz Cheddar cheese, grated
2 slices of bread
2 generous tsp mango chutney
2 tsp softened butter or mayonnaise

Heat the oil in a cast iron or non-stick frying pan or skillet over a medium-high flame and add the chickpeas. Fry, shaking the pan at regular intervals, until crispy and brown. Add the spices and pinch of salt and cook for another minute or so. Tip into a bowl and add the onion, chilli, coriander and cheese, and stir to combine evenly.

Wipe the pan clean. Spread both slices of bread with the mango chutney. Top one slice with the filling, then finish with the second slice of bread and press down lightly. Spread the outsides, top and bottom, with the butter or mayonnaise, then fry for 3–4 minutes on each side in your pan, with a gentle weight on top, until crispy, golden and oozing.

TRUFFLED TUNWORTH AND PICKLED WALNUT TOASTIE

This is ridiculously opulent – less a lunch, more of a full cheese course or, if you are that way inclined, a savoury to be eaten around midnight at the mid- to tail-end of what can really only be described as 'a session'. Have it prepared in advance and it will require very little mental acuity to complete.

SERVES 1, THOUGH CONSIDER MAKING MORE

¼ tsp good black truffle paste
30g/1oz softened butter
2 slices of day-old bread – brioche works particularly well
60–75g/2¼–2¾oz Tunworth cheese or Camembert, thickly sliced
1 small pickled walnut, very thinly sliced

Beat the truffle paste into half of the butter and spread it on one slice of the bread. Lay your sliced cheese on the other slice. Top the cheese with the pickled walnut. Assemble the sandwich. Spread the remaining butter on the outsides, top and bottom. Wrap and chill until required.

Put a non-stick frying or cast iron pan over a medium-high heat. Cook the unwrapped sandwich for 3–4 minutes on each side until golden, oozing and irresistible. Cut it into triangles, enjoying the ASMR as you do so. Eat.

Smoked cod's roe on toast

There was for a time – though I think it has passed – the sense that there was an unwritten rule mandating that any new Eurocentric restaurant in London serve smoked cod's roe as a snack. I was absolutely fine with this state of affairs, because smoked cod's roe is almost never not delicious.

I am indebted to Feri Nemcsik at the fabulous Parsons in Covent Garden for this recipe. Naturally I am biased, considering my involvement in the kitchen at Parsons' sister restaurant, The 10 Cases, but Parsons is the best fish restaurant in town and Feri is a mensch. Thank you for the recipe, chef.

SERVES 6 AS A STARTER

100g/3½oz crustless stale bread (save the crusts for chapters 4 and 5)
160ml/5½fl oz water
100ml/3½fl oz fresh lemon juice
150g/5½oz fresh cod's roe, skinned
2 small garlic cloves, crushed
25g/1oz shallot, roughly chopped
Zest of 1 lemon
A pinch of cayenne pepper
10g/¼oz salt
500ml/18fl oz vegetable oil
Toasted sourdough or warm flatbreads, to serve

Soak the stale bread in the water and lemon juice for 10 minutes. Blend with the remaining ingredients, except for the oil, until smooth. Slowly add the oil with the blender running, until you reach a good consistency. Check for seasoning and adjust with lemon or salt if required.

Serve with sourdough toast or warm flatbreads.

Crab and radish on toast

Buy, cook and pick a whole crab if that's your jam.
I usually can't be bothered.

SERVES 4 AS A LIGHT LUNCH OR STARTER

50g/1¾oz brown crab meat
50g/1¾oz softened butter
Pinch of chilli flakes
A little grated nutmeg
150g/5½oz white crab meat
40g/1½oz mayonnaise
2 tbsp lemon juice, plus extra to serve
100g/3½oz breakfast radishes
4 slices of sourdough
1 garlic clove, halved
Extra virgin olive oil
Sea salt and freshly ground black pepper

Beat together the brown crab meat, butter, chilli and nutmeg until smooth.

Mix together the white crab meat, mayonnaise and lemon juice. Season
with sea salt and black pepper and check for seasoning. Add more salt or
lemon juice if required.

Wash the radishes, then slice them thinly. Keep the leaves.

Toast your bread. Rub it with the garlic. Spread it with the brown crab
butter. Top it with the white crab mayonnaise, then the sliced radishes, then
the radish tops, before finishing with a swizzle of extra virgin olive oil and a
squeeze of lemon.

Goat's curd, raw peas and herbs

A dish for summer's height, but one to enjoy before the peas have become too large, bullet-like and mealy. You will need twice as many pods as you think because you will eat half of the peas while podding. This is just scientific fact.

While this dish is recommended as an elegant little starter, you could quite happily repurpose it as a side to lamb, ideally with the addition of black olives and a half-decent bottle of Syrah. A few thyme- and garlic-heavy roasted tomatoes in the mix and you're really cooking on gas.

If you can't find goat's curd, tie up a muslin/cheesecloth filled with goat's milk yogurt over a bowl for 12 hours and strain out the whey. Same difference, really.

SERVES 4

300g/10½oz pea pods
A good handful of mixed delicate herbs – such as young parsley leaves,
    chervil, finely chopped chives, amaranth, basil cress, fennel fronds, mint
    – a few of the above
4 slices of sourdough
½ garlic clove
200g/7oz goat's curd
Olive oil
½ lemon
Sea salt and freshly ground black pepper

Pod the peas. Control yourself. Try one, though. If they are at the larger end of the spectrum, blanch them in boiling salted water for 2 minutes before plunging them into iced water. Drain well and keep them handy.

Pick down the herbs, discarding as many stems as you have the energy for. Toss together.

Toast the bread. Rub it with the cut garlic. Spread with the goat's curd. Top with the peas and then the herbs. Finish with olive oil, a squeeze of lemon, a good pinch of sea salt and a twist of black pepper.

Scotch woodcock

This dish has somewhat patrician connotations that might make some disinclined to consider it. Mrs. Beeton provides a recipe in her *Cookery and Household Management* (1861), though, unlike some more conscientious writers, she couldn't be bothered to offer an explanation by way of introduction. Unbelievable. Anyway, the Victorians were fond of it and it was a House of Commons standard well into the twentieth century. Today you can find it in the clubs of St. James's as a 'savoury' – that's to say, an alternative to pudding or cheese.

So yes, it's something of a relic, but a delicious one, and ludicrously easy to throw together. Oh, and it doesn't contain woodcock. Rather like Welsh rarebit containing no rabbit, this contains no woodcock. Those Victorians, what a hoot.

SERVES 2

75g/2¾oz softened butter
4 eggs, beaten
2 slices of sourdough
8 anchovy fillets
8 lilliput capers
Salt and freshly ground black pepper

Melt 50g/1¾oz or so of the butter in a heavy-bottomed saucepan over a medium-low heat. Add the eggs and gently start to scramble, stirring frequently to achieve smallish curds (the lower the heat and the more infrequent the stirring, the larger the curds, and vice versa). Season with salt and pepper towards the end of cooking.

While your eggs are scrambling, toast the bread. Spread with the remaining butter. Top with the scrambled eggs. Arrange the anchovy fillets and capers artfully on top. Finish with a little more pepper. Eat.

Snails and lardo on toast

This has been on and off the menu at The 10 Cases, where I work as some sort of nebulous hybrid of food director and kitchen dogsbody, since I began there in 2020. Being a French bistro I felt we needed snails on the menu, though I couldn't resist adding a little top-spin in the form of salted pig fat. Molluscs go with pork, right?

If serving pescatarians, or vegetarians who don't mind a little garden protein, use butter instead of lardo. If not, consider this a terrific garnish to a steak.

You can get canned snails online very easily indeed. Never look back. Should you not be able to get hold of lardo, Brindisa's Iberico pig fat is easy to track down in large supermarkets and online.

SERVES 4

A good handful of parsley leaves
A good handful of watercress, plus optional extra to garnish
150g/5½oz lardo, skinned and cubed
½ tsp finely chopped rosemary
1 garlic clove, crushed
½ tsp chilli flakes
1 tsp red wine vinegar
A can of snails (32–40 in total), drained and rinsed
4 slices of sourdough
Salt and espelette pepper or freshly ground black pepper

Bring a pan of lightly salted water to the boil and add the parsley and watercress. Blanch for 30 seconds, drain, and plunge into very cold water to set the colour. Squeeze out all the water and blend with the lardo, rosemary, garlic, chilli and vinegar until smooth and verdant.

When ready to eat, melt half the lardo and herb mixture in a pan over a medium heat and add the snails. Season with a pinch of salt and cook for 5 minutes or so, stirring regularly, until hot.

Toast the bread and spread with the remaining lardo. Top with the snails and dust with espelette pepper. Garnish with watercress if you like. Eat hot.

Prawn toast

At some point the thought occurred to me to do a fish version of coq au vin, poaching monkfish in chicken stock and serving it with a red wine reduction, lardons, mushrooms, baby onions and so on. And then, instead of croutons, prawn toast. Here's the prawn toast element. We made a mayonnaise using roasted prawn head oil, which might be a step too far, but if you're interested: roast the prawn heads for 5 minutes in a hot oven, blend with vegetable oil, pass through a muslin-lined sieve, and use the oil to make a mayonnaise.

Serve as a snack/canapé.

MAKES 30 TOASTS

300g/10½oz raw prawns, shells and heads removed
30g/1oz egg white
A pinch of chilli flakes, to taste
A good pinch of salt
2 tbsp chopped chives
30 slices of baguette, or equivalent-sized pieces of sourdough
150g/5½oz dried breadcrumbs
250ml/9fl oz vegetable oil
Lemon wedges, to serve

In a food processor, pulse the prawns, egg white, chilli flakes and salt until it comes together. Don't over-blend – you want some texture to the prawns.

Fold through the chives, then fry a little of the mix and taste for seasoning. Remember that if it's going to be served as a snack it needs to be at the saltier end of the spectrum.

Spread the mix on the pieces of bread. Dip each piece, prawn-side down, into the breadcrumbs to coat thoroughly. Cover and chill until ready.

Heat the oil in a sauté pan or wok and fry a few pieces at a time for a minute or two on each side until crisp and golden. Serve with wedges of lemon.

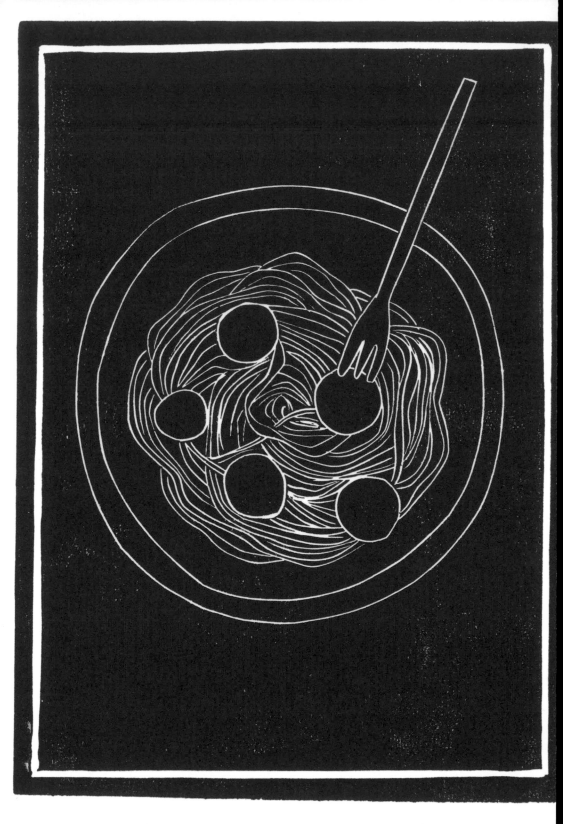

DAY THREE

Salads & So On...

As we get into the third day in the life of your loaf you may start to detect a staleness that makes you less inclined to nibble idly at the bread or simply dip it in olive oil. Action needs taking, and that action should not be to throw the bread in the bin – there is still a great deal of fun to be had with this loaf. The previous chapter with its ideas on toast remains entirely available to you here, though equally you may want to start thinking about other options – croutons for salads, dishes whose toast element asks for a crisper, drier kind of toast, or with something juicy that can seep into the bread. We're not quite at the full rehydration stage of the next chapter, but you won't be able to knock up a sandwich without noticing a distinct lack of moisture. In short, we are on the precipice, in that liminal phase between youth and senescence. What you have here is a middle-aged loaf of bread with a lot to offer the world.

A simple chicken salad

A proper chicken salad shouldn't be so much a salad as a spectacular profusion of deliciousness with a few leaves thrown in for colour and vitamin C. Yes, and flavour and texture, too, but ultimately the focus here is not so much on the salad as the chicken, and perhaps the dressing, which delivers a good mustard punch, and certainly the croutons, which are the point of this book.

Here I've included oak-smoked Isle of Wight tomatoes – I've found big supermarkets tend to stock them. They are marvellous if you can get them but entirely optional.

SERVES 4

For the dressing
1 egg yolk
1 generous tbsp Dijon mustard
1 small garlic clove, minced
A few good shakes of Tabasco sauce
2 tbsp red wine vinegar
6 tbsp light olive or groundnut/peanut oil
Salt and freshly ground black pepper

For the salad
3 tbsp olive oil
1 garlic clove, unpeeled and just lightly pressed
A sprig of thyme
200g/7oz two-day-old bread, roughly torn
2 heads of Gem lettuce leaves
60g/2¼oz watercress
400g/14oz cooked chicken, shredded
20g/¾oz flat-leaf parsley, leaves only
1 finely chopped shallot
1 small tub of smoked Isle of Wight tomatoes, drained (optional)
1 tbsp finely chopped chives
Salt

First make the dressing by whisking together the egg yolk, mustard, garlic, Tabasco and vinegar, and then slowly adding the oil while you whisk. Season with salt and black pepper.

Make the croutons for the salad by heating the olive oil in a frying pan or skillet. Add the garlic and thyme and fry for a minute or so, then add the bread and continue to cook, stirring regularly, until crisp and golden. Season with salt.

Arrange the lettuce and watercress in a serving bowl or on individual plates. Top with the chicken, croutons, parsley, shallot, smoked tomatoes (if using) and chives.

Dress excessively and serve swiftly.

Fatt-ish

This is my take on fattoush – a Levantine salad – in almost all but name, fattoush being traditionally made using stale flatbreads (which you can of course use here), though in keeping with the drift of this book I'm making this with a loaf, which may or may not get me in hot water.

Serve with grilled lamb or chicken.

SERVES 6 AS A SIDE

For the croutons
200–300g/7–10½oz stale bread, roughly torn
4 tbsp olive oil

For the dressing
½ garlic clove, crushed
Juice of 1 lemon
100ml/3½fl oz olive oil
½ tsp sumac
½ tsp chilli flakes
1 tsp honey
A pinch of salt

For the rest
500g/1lb 2oz ripe tomatoes
1 cucumber or 3 small ones
3 spring onions/scallions
A small bunch of radishes, with their tops
A good handful of picked parsley leaves
Sumac, to finish

Preheat the oven to 180°C fan/200°C/400°F/gas mark 6.

Toss together the torn bread and the olive oil, then bake on a tray for 10–12 minutes until crisp and golden but not altogether dried out.

Meanwhile, put all the dressing ingredients in a jar and shake to emulsify.

Roughly chop the tomatoes, cucumber and spring onions. Separate the radishes from their leaves and wash both. Halve or, if they're especially large, quarter the radishes.

In a large and handsome serving bowl toss together the vegetables, radish leaves, herbs, dressing and croutons. Finish with a generous sprinkling of sumac.

Kale Caesar

The chef Florence Knight used to produce a salad of burnt bread, raw cavolo nero and anchovy at the much-missed Polpetto restaurant in Soho that was eye-openingly bold, ambitious and indeed delicious. Here I blanch the leaves, but do keep them raw if you'd prefer.

SERVES 4 AS A STARTER

For the dressing
1 egg yolk
1 tbsp Dijon mustard
1 small garlic clove, minced
2 anchovy fillets
A few shakes of Tabasco sauce
2 tbsp red wine or sherry vinegar
4 tbsp light olive or groundnut/peanut oil
Freshly ground black pepper

For the rest
300g/10½oz kale leaves – curly, purple, cavolo nero – take your pick
150g/5½oz bread, roughly torn
2 tbsp olive oil
12 anchovy fillets
Parmesan cheese
½ lemon

Make the dressing by blending together all of the ingredients except the oil in a food processor, then slowly add the oil until smooth and emulsified. Season with black pepper.

Strip the kale from its stems and roughly chop, discarding the stems. Bring a deep pan of lightly salted water to the boil and blanch the kale briefly – max. 1 minute. Drain and plunge into iced water. Drain again and gently squeeze out all the water, then dry thoroughly in a salad spinner.

Fry the bread in the olive oil until crisp and golden. Toss the kale with the dressing and croutons and serve with the anchovy fillets, a good grating of Parmesan and a squeeze of lemon.

Steak and eggs

One of the few instances in which a steak for breakfast is justifiable.
Eat with strong coffee.

SERVES 1

200g/7oz rib-eye steak
1 tsp groundnut/peanut oil
50g/1¾oz rustic bread, roughly torn
1 tbsp butter
2 eggs
1 tsp very finely chopped green chilli
A shake of chipotle chilli flakes (optional)
A handful of coriander/cilantro leaves
½ lime
Sea salt and freshly ground black pepper

Get a heavy-bottomed frying pan or skillet good and hot. Rub the steak
with the oil and season well with salt and pepper. Cook for 3–4 minutes on
each side, then remove to a warm plate to rest.

Add the bread to the pan and fry in the rendered beef fat until golden and
crisp. Season with a little sea salt and remove.

Add the butter to the pan and let it skid and fizz around until the foam
subsides, then add the eggs. Fry for a couple of minutes until crisp
underneath and just set on top.

Slice the steak and plate with the fried eggs and croutons. Finish with the
chopped chilli, chipotle flakes if using, coriander and a squeeze of lime.

Four French toasts

As kids we always called this eggy bread, but let's be honest, French toast sounds more appealing. Here are four ways with this old favourite.

CLASSIC

The basic French toast for when you haven't the time, inclination or perhaps the ingredients to muck about.

SERVES 1

1 egg
2 tbsp whole milk
1 slice of two-day-old bread – sourdough or brioche works well
A knob of butter

To serve
1 tbsp granulated sugar
½ tsp ground cinnamon

Whisk the egg and milk in a shallow dish. Add the bread and leave to soak for 5 minutes, turning halfway through.

Melt the butter over a medium-high heat in a frying pan or skillet until foaming. Cook the eggy bread for 3–4 minutes on each side until golden.

Meanwhile, mix the sugar and cinnamon on a plate. Turn the cooked toast in it to coat thoroughly. Eat.

BACON AND BANANA

Shameless, yes. Delicious, absolutely. The thicker cut your bacon, the better.

SERVES 1

All the above, plus:
A few slices of thick-cut streaky bacon (smoked, preferably)
1 banana, sliced
Maple syrup

Cook the French toast as in the classic recipe, omitting the cinnamon sugar. Meanwhile, fry or grill/broil the bacon until crisp. Briefly toss the banana in the bacon fat until warmed through. Top the toast with the banana, bacon and a splash of maple syrup.

GRILLED PEACH, STRACCIATELLA AND MINT

This is one of those hybrid dishes that can't quite make up its mind if it's sweet or savoury and is therefore very much A Brunch Dish. Throw some prosciutto into the mix if you fancy.

Stracciatella is a type of cheese similar to burrata and not the easiest to come by – replace happily with burrata itself, mozzarella, or even thick yogurt.

SERVES 1

All the above, plus:
1 peach, stoned and quartered
Olive oil
25g/1oz stracciatella cheese
A few mint leaves
Balsamic vinegar

Make the French toast as in the classic recipe, omitting the cinnamon sugar. Meanwhile, get a griddle pan good and hot. Toss the peach quarters in the olive oil and then griddle for a couple of minutes on each side until charred and starting to yield.

Serve on the French toast topped with stracciatella, torn mint and a splash of good balsamic vinegar.

FRENCH TOAST ICE-CREAM SANDWICH WITH MISO BUTTERSCOTCH

A level of decadence up from the bacon and banana episode. Shop-bought ice cream all the way, though if you wanted to double-carb you could of course use the brown bread ice-cream recipe on page 122.

SERVES 1

All the above, plus:
2 tsp white miso
2 tbsp butter
1 tbsp soft light brown sugar
1 tsp sake (optional)
½ tsp sherry vinegar
Vanilla ice cream

In a small saucepan cook the miso over a medium-high heat, stirring almost constantly, until it starts to take on colour. Keep going – you want it good and brown. Add the butter and brown sugar and stir until the butter has melted. Add the sake, if using, and vinegar, and simmer gently for 5 minutes. Keep warm.

Make the French toast as in the classic recipe, including the coating of cinnamon sugar. Slice the French toast in half. Take a large scoop of ice cream and deposit it on one half. Spoon over the butterscotch. Top with the other half of toast and eat as elegantly as you can manage.

Chicken liver pâté with melba toast

It doesn't get much more Barbara Cartland than melba toast. Although it has fallen out of fashion and favour, all it takes is one trip to the great Oslo Court restaurant in the heart of St John's Wood to remind you of the importance of melba toast. It's a vehicle for all kinds of deliciousness, and a fitting farewell for a stale loaf.

SERVES 4

4 slices of stale bread

For the pâté
100g/3½oz unsalted butter at room temperature
1 garlic clove, finely minced
1 banana shallot, finely chopped
200g/7oz chicken livers, trimmed
2 sprigs of thyme
A splash of brandy
Salt and freshly ground black pepper
50g/1¾oz melted butter, to finish
Chutney, to serve (optional)

Preheat the oven to 160°C fan/180°C/350°F/gas mark 4.

Toast the bread, then remove the crusts (save for other purposes, of course) and cut through each slice horizontally to make eight thin slices of toast. Scrape away any excess doughy bits, then cut the bread into triangles or whatever shape blows your hair back. Put in the oven and bake for 8–10 minutes until crisp and dry.

To make the pâté, melt a quarter or so of the butter in a sauté pan or skillet and gently cook the garlic and shallot until soft – about 15 minutes. Add the chicken livers and thyme, season well with salt and pepper and cook over a medium heat for 5–8 minutes, stirring occasionally, until firm but not overcooked. Add the brandy and simmer for a further minute to cook off the excess alcohol – you can use a flame to speed this up if you enjoy such high jinks.

Add the remaining room-temperature butter and leave to soften off the heat for a few minutes, then blend everything in a food processor. Pass through a fine sieve into a bowl, then transfer to a sterilized jar or serving dish. Top with the melted butter and leave until cool, then refrigerate.

Serve with the melba toast and perhaps a little chutney. Pretend it's 1985.

Garlic bread with gorgonzola, truffle and mushrooms

As kids we used to have garlic bread with pasta as standard – supermarket garlic bread, occasionally forgotten about in the oven to the point of being identifiable only by its dental records. It was as if pasta's relatively recent ubiquity was still met with some scepticism, and back-up carbs were required. Several decades later, in our carb-wary way, this seems totally perverse but, boy, was it good at the time. Something about scooping bolognese sauce onto pungent garlic bread made perfect sense.

So, yeah, go on, serve this with pasta. Or eat alone, late at night. Your shout. Both work.

SERVES 8–10

25g/1oz butter
3–4 flat mushrooms, sliced
2 tsp chopped thyme leaves
400g/14oz gorgonzola piccante
8 garlic cloves, minced
½ tsp truffle paste (optional)
A good handful of finely chopped parsley
1 sourdough loaf, or 2 baguettes
Salt and freshly ground black pepper

Preheat the oven to 180°C fan/200°C/400°F/gas mark 6.

Melt the butter over a medium heat, then add the mushrooms and thyme and season with salt. Cook, stirring occasionally, for 5 minutes until softened. Set aside.

Blend the gorgonzola in a food processor with the garlic, truffle paste if using, parsley and several twists of black pepper.

Take the bread and slice it almost all the way through to the bottom to create the familiar garlic bread concertina. Fill each crevasse with the gorgonzola and garlic paste and a few mushroom slices. Rub the loaf all over with cold water. Wrap in foil and bake for 20 minutes. Remove the foil and bake for a further 5 minutes. Serve.

Pickled herring

Lidl supermarket has some absolutely killer herring. They come in small tubs in a cream sauce with apple, gherkin and dill and I'm mildly obsessed. There is guaranteed to be some tucked away in the fridge at my in-laws and I have to confess to micro-dosing the stuff throughout the day when I think no one is looking. I tear a hunk of sourdough from the bread bin that is conveniently located above the fridge, then crouch down pretending to search for mustard or butter or some other essential. It is then the work of an instant to ease the lid off the herring, scoop out the already conveniently chopped up fish and its sauce, and thumb it into my mouth. My wife finds the whole process mildly repellent.

This version is almost as delicious as the Lidl effort. The bread vehicle for this is pretty versatile – you could go with some melba toast (page 62), toasted rye or fresh sourdough. I've no idea why it's in this chapter but it's as good as any, I suppose.

SERVES 4

250ml/9fl oz water
250ml/9fl oz white wine vinegar
100g/3½oz sugar
30g/1oz salt
1 bay leaf
1 tsp coriander seeds
1 tsp black peppercorns
4 herring (or small mackerel) fillets, pin-boned and trimmed
200ml/7fl oz double/heavy cream
200g/7oz sour cream
1 apple, peeled, cored and diced
1 small red onion, finely diced
1 gherkin, diced
2 tbsp chopped dill fronds
Bread or toast, to serve

Put the water, vinegar, sugar and salt into a pan and bring to the boil, stirring to dissolve the sugar. Add the bay leaf and spices and simmer for 5 minutes, then leave to cool completely. Pour over the herring fillets and leave, covered, for 24 hours in the fridge.

Mix the creams, apple, onion, gherkin and dill. Drain the herring, reserving the pickling liquor for now. Slice into 3cm/1¼in pieces, then mix with the cream dressing. Taste for seasoning and add a little of the pickling liquor if you feel it needs sharpening up.

Serve with bread or toast as preferred. It will keep, covered, in the fridge for five days.

Sage and anchovy soldiers

For this recipe I am indebted to Rowley Leigh, whose deserving-of-the-word iconic Parmesan custard with anchovy soldiers remains one of the more exciting and original creations of the past few decades of British cooking, as far as I can tell.

This consolidates things into one excellent place. Serve either as finger snacks or as an accompaniment to soup.

MAKES 18 SOLDIERS

6 large, thin slices of sourdough
1½ tbsp Dijon mustard
25g/1oz anchovy fillets
3 sage leaves, finely chopped
1 small garlic clove, minced
30g/1oz Parmesan cheese, grated
Olive oil, if required
Butter, for frying
Freshly ground black pepper

Lightly roll out the bread slices to make them a little thinner if necessary. You're aiming for 1cm/½in thickness.

Put the mustard, anchovies, sage, garlic and Parmesan in a food processor and blend until smooth, adding a little olive oil to help it along if necessary. Season generously with black pepper.

Divide the mix between 3 slices of bread and press the other slices down on top to sandwich the filling.

Melt a little butter in a frying pan or skillet over a medium heat. Fry the sandwiches for 3–4 minutes on each side, with something heavy on top to compress, until golden and crisp. Slice each into 6 soldiers, and eat.

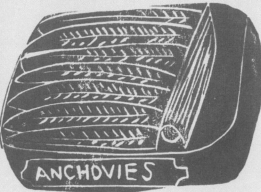

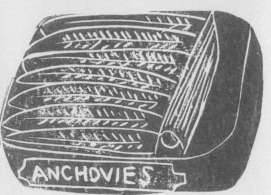

Spaghetti and meatballs

This could absolutely find its way into a later chapter and be made with bread that is considerably more stale. Let's not split hairs.

SERVES 4–6

50g/1¾oz old bread, roughly torn
50ml/2fl oz whole milk
350g/12oz minced/ground beef, not too lean
2 tbsp raisins, roughly chopped
2 tbsp toasted pine nuts, roughly chopped
2 tbsp parsley, finely chopped
2 tbsp finely grated Parmesan cheese, plus extra to serve
½ tsp garlic powder
2 tbsp olive oil
2 tbsp tomato purée/paste
400g/14oz can chopped tomatoes
A good handful of basil
500g/1lb 2oz spaghetti
Salt and freshly ground black pepper

Soak the bread in the milk for 10 minutes. Gently squeeze out the milk so the bread isn't totally soggy, then break up into a large mixing bowl. Add the beef, raisins, pine nuts, parsley, Parmesan, a good pinch of salt and the garlic powder and gently work everything together. Don't over-massage or you'll have tough meatballs. Shape into golf-ball-sized meatballs, cover and chill for an hour if possible – overnight even better. While not essential by any means, chilling helps the meatballs keep their shape when you cook them.

In a large sauté pan or saucepan, fry the meatballs in the olive oil over a medium-high heat until well browned – the key is not to turn them until you have a really good crust. When you're satisfied with the colour, add the tomato purée and stir briefly, then add the chopped tomatoes and perhaps half the basil. Season with salt, then gently simmer, uncovered, stirring occasionally.

Meanwhile, bring a deep pan of salted water to the boil and cook your spaghetti according to the packet instructions. Drain the spaghetti, reserving some water in a small jug, just in case.

Toss together the spaghetti and meatballs, adding a little pasta water if required to loosen it up a little. Serve in warmed bowls with black pepper and Parmesan and sprinkled with the remaining basil.

Chocolate and cherry bread and butter pudding

Bread and butter pudding is one of those endlessly adaptable staples with which you can't go too far wrong. I like it with panettone or hot cross buns or croissants, but given the nature of this book those felt a little off-topic. Don't hesitate to gild the lily with any of those, should you have them handy.

This is best prepared a day or two in advance of baking, though that's not essential. I've put this recipe here, as opposed to in the next chapter with the other bread puddings, because I felt the richness of the chocolate encourages a slightly lighter, less stodgy bread … but it very possibly doesn't matter either way.

SERVES 8–10

100g/3½oz dried cherries
5 tbsp bourbon
1 tbsp kirsch or other cherry liqueur (optional)
500g/1lb 2oz sliced bread (crustless if you prefer), cut into quarters
200g/7oz dark chocolate
100g/3½oz butter, plus extra for greasing
500ml/18fl oz double/heavy cream
125g/4½oz caster/superfine sugar
½ tsp ground allspice
4 eggs

Soak the cherries in the bourbon and kirsch (if using) and leave for 30 minutes or so.

Butter the inside of a baking dish, about 30 x 22cm/12 x 9in (aka Ikea special). Arrange the sliced bread in the dish, scattering the cherries amid the quarters.

Break up the chocolate into a heatproof bowl set over a pan of gently simmering water and add the butter, cream, sugar and allspice. When the chocolate and butter have melted, give it all a good stir to bring it together.

Break the eggs into a separate large bowl. Pour over your chocolate cream, whisking as you do. Now pour this over the bread. Cover and chill for a minimum of 12 hours.

Bake for 40–45 minutes at 160°C fan/180°C/350°F/gas mark 4 until hot throughout. Serve with cold double cream, or ice cream.

DAY FOUR

Crusts

Now that your bread is past even the stage whereby you can just about revivify it with a splash of water and 10 minutes in a hot oven, you should start to think of ways to maximize its utility without having to go full breadcrumb. This is where soups start to assert themselves in my mind – there's something about the way an aged loaf inhabits good broth that is perfectly symbiotic, the broth giving life to the bread, enhancing its savouriness, creating a texture that is somehow both pappy and comforting; the bread in turn bringing a yeasty, sour complexity to the broth. A silk purse from a sow's ear.

Throw a panzanella into the mix, a few savoury bread puddings, and a nifty way with roast chicken and you're well set for the last throw of the dice before pulling out the food processor and making breadcrumbs.

Panzanella

What often gets forgotten about panzanella is that it's a bread salad – it's not a tomato salad with a few lonely croutons. Go big on the bread. If, when you've finished eating this, you feel like you've eaten a salad, you've probably done it wrong.

Frugal as this is in theory, for it to be truly knock-out you need premier-league tomatoes, bread and olive oil, which don't come cheap, at least not in the UK. And people wonder why the River Café is expensive.

I've put this recipe here because, unlike the croutons in the previous chapter – where a bit of chew and some hot crispness is preferable – this recipe requires soaking the stale bread in the tomato juices. If you are using fresher bread – and there's no good reason not to – toss it in oil first and bake in a hot oven for 5 minutes until crisp.

This is very simple but – in an ideal world – needs beginning a couple of hours before eating.

SERVES 4–6

1kg/2lb 4oz tomatoes – the best you can find
2 tsp flaked sea salt
100ml/3½fl oz good olive oil
2 tbsp white wine vinegar (or, if you want a little kick, the brine from
   a jar of pickled jalapeños)
400g/14oz chunky croutons – sourdough for preference
½ red onion, very thinly sliced
A handful of torn basil leaves
A light grating of Parmesan cheese

I hesitate to instruct you to peel the tomatoes. It's a hassle. But peel them if you like (sharp knife, cross in the bottom, pour over boiling water, sit for a minute, drain, peel). It will make this a better salad.

Roughly chop the tomatoes into handsome chunks, saving all the juices, and toss with the salt, olive oil and vinegar. Leave to macerate for 1–2 hours.

Sit a colander over a bowl containing your stale bread croutons. Tip the tomatoes into the colander and lightly press to extract a little more juice, then give the bread pieces a toss, leaving them in the tomato dressing for at least 20 minutes, up to 2 hours.

To finish, combine the soaked bread with the tomatoes, red onion and basil, and dust with Parmesan.

Pappa al pomodoro

I always feel this is the autumnal yin to panzanella's summery yang. There is deep comfort within and it's the kind of dish that tempts the writer – like a flighted off-break outside the off stump tempts the batter – to wheel out the tired cliché 'humble'.

The food writer Jonathan Nunn once said: 'It's my strong belief that Italian soups are the most underrated part of Italian cuisine. How can you not respect a soup which is about 80% olive oil and at least 10% melted cheese?'

The ratio here may disappoint Jonathan but the spirit of the thing – as with the Ribollita on page 82 – is in full agreement.

SERVES 4–6

4 tbsp olive oil, plus extra to serve
2 garlic cloves, unpeeled and just lightly crushed
½ onion, peeled
500g/1lb 2oz peeled tomatoes (see the previous recipe)
500g/1lb 2oz quality canned tomatoes
300g/10½oz stale bread, torn into chunks
A good handful of basil leaves, roughly torn
White wine vinegar, to taste
Salt and freshly ground black pepper
Parmesan cheese, to serve

Heat the oil in a large pan over a medium heat and add the garlic and onion. Fry, shuggling the pan occasionally, and allow to colour a little over the course of 5 minutes or so. Remove the onion and garlic and discard.

Add the fresh and canned tomatoes along with 250ml/9fl oz water, season with salt and gently cook over a low heat for 30 minutes, stirring occasionally. Add the bread and basil and gently simmer for a further 15 minutes. Taste and add a little more salt, some pepper and a splash of vinegar if required. You may want to let it down with a little more water too, though you'll need to adjust the seasoning accordingly.

Serve with a generous few sloshes of olive oil and grated Parmesan.

French onion soup

More important than the onions here is the quality and depth of the stock.
I'm not necessarily suggesting that you have to make your own – though
by all means do if you have the time and the bandwidth – but try to buy
the best you can get your hands on. It needs to be rich, dark, robust and
overwhelmingly savoury. If you're using vegetable stock (not, strictly,
recommended) then add a dash of Maggi Liquid Seasoning to give it
some welly.

SERVES 4–6

50g/1¾oz butter
1kg/2lb 4oz brown onions, sliced
2 tsp thyme leaves
200ml/7fl oz dry oloroso sherry or marsala
1.5 litres/1½ quarts rich chicken or beef stock
150g/5½oz stale baguette or sourdough, roughly torn
100g/3½oz Gruyère cheese, grated
Salt and freshly ground black pepper

Melt the butter over a low heat in a heavy-bottomed saucepan and add
the onions and thyme leaves. Season with salt and cook for 45 minutes to
1 hour, stirring occasionally, until the onions are golden and melting – take
care not to colour too dramatically or the whole thing gets a little bitter.

Bring up the temperature to medium-high and add the sherry. Simmer for
a couple of minutes, then add the stock. Bring back to a simmer and leave
for 5 minutes or so. Taste for seasoning and adjust if necessary.

Divide the bread between the required number of (ovenproof) soup bowls
and spoon over the soup. Sprinkle over the Gruyère, then place under the
grill/broiler for a few minutes until the cheese is bubbling and golden.

Season with black pepper and serve.

Garbure

It's unclear whether there is any connection between 'garbure' and 'garbage', though in many ways I would encourage you – in the best way possible – to consider this dish a good use of odds and ends in the fridge. This isn't so much to disrespect the dish, as to respect the vegetable matter you have that may otherwise end up in the compost.

This is a Gascon dish that traditionally would contain confit of goose, though I use ham hock here, which is far from controversial.

SERVES 4–6

50g/1¾oz butter
1 onion, roughly chopped
4 garlic cloves, roughly chopped
2 celery sticks, roughly chopped
2 carrots, roughly chopped
1 glass of white wine
2 litres/2 quarts chicken stock
1 large ham hock, smoked or unsmoked (your call)
1 bouquet garni
8 baby turnips, halved
1 Savoy cabbage, sliced
150g/5½oz stale bread, torn into chunks
Salt and freshly ground black pepper

Melt the butter in a large pan and add the onion, garlic, celery and carrot. Season with salt and pepper, cover and gently cook for 20 minutes or so until softened. Add the wine and simmer for a couple of minutes, then add the stock and ham hock. Bring to the boil and skim off any grey matter that appears on the surface. Add the bouquet garni, cover and gently simmer for 2 hours, or until the meat is falling off the bone.

Remove the ham and strip the meat, then return it to the pot along with the turnips, cabbage and bread. Simmer for 10 minutes or until the vegetables are cooked and the broth has thickened. Check for seasoning and serve.

Ribollita

Many years ago I spent several months working on a farm in the middle of Tuscany. I had gone there to work as a chef but it was decided my skill levels were, ah, somewhere below what was required, and so I was turfed into the garden to plant herbs, feed pigs and slaughter the occasional rooster (I vacuum-packed its testicles and put them in the freezer as a prank. Good times…).

Lunches in the dusky and dusty workmen's shed were surprisingly jolly affairs and where I learned most of the Italian I have since forgotten. I would like to say that they involved steaming tureens of ribollita washed down with tumblers of rough local wine, followed by an argument about the correct time of year to eat *lampredotto*, and then a siesta, but I can't remember. Let's agree that's what happened.

SERVES 4–6

4 tbsp olive oil
2 onions, roughly chopped
2 celery sticks, trimmed and finely chopped
2 carrots, diced
4 garlic cloves, chopped
400g/14oz can cannellini beans, drained and rinsed
400g/14oz can chopped tomatoes
1 bay leaf
300g/10½oz stale bread, roughly torn
1 glass of (rough local) red wine
1.5 litres/generous 1½ quarts dark chicken stock,
　　or good vegetable stock
250g/9oz cavolo nero, de-stemmed and roughly chopped
Salt and freshly ground black pepper

To serve
Your best olive oil
Parmesan cheese

Heat the oil in a large pan and gently fry the root vegetables and garlic until softened – about 20 minutes. Season with salt and pepper. Add the beans, tomatoes, bay leaf, bread and wine, and simmer for 5 minutes, then add the stock. Bring back to a simmer and leave to tick over for a further 20 minutes until thickened.

Add the cavolo nero and simmer to desired *cuisson*. If you like it fresh and crunchy, just a couple of minutes. I prefer it well cooked in this instance so would cook it for more like 10–15 minutes. Your dinner, your call.

Serve with a profligate amount of olive oil, a good dusting of Parmesan, and pepper and salt as required.

Garlic soup

Across eastern Europe – though also notably in Spain – a garlic soup of one stripe or another is employed as the ultimate hangover cure. This is an entirely inauthentic iteration of that head-clearing elixir.

SERVES 4

2 garlic bulbs
2 tbsp olive oil
200g/7oz stale bread – sourdough or rye – cubed
50g/1¾oz butter
1 celery stick, diced
A sprig of thyme
1 tsp coriander seeds
½ tsp chilli flakes
500g/1lb 2oz waxy potatoes, peeled and cubed
1.2 litres/1¼ quarts chicken or vegetable stock
2 eggs, beaten
Sea salt and freshly ground black pepper
2 tbsp finely chopped parsley, to serve

Preheat the oven to 160°C fan/180°C/350°F/gas mark 4.

Separate and peel the cloves from one bulb of garlic. Set aside.

Trim the top off the other bulb. Drizzle with 1 tablespoon of the olive oil, season with a pinch of sea salt, and wrap in foil. Put the bread in a baking tray, toss with the other tablespoon of olive oil, then put in the oven, along with the garlic bulb. After 5 minutes, remove the bread. Leave the garlic to bake for a further 40 minutes. When tender and sweet, remove from the oven and leave to cool, then squeeze the cloves out of the papery skins.

Meanwhile, melt the butter in a large pan over a low heat. Mince your reserved garlic cloves and cook very gently, stirring regularly, for 10 minutes until just a little coloured and cooked through. Add the celery, thyme, coriander seeds, chilli flakes and potatoes. Season well, stir to combine, then add the stock and bring to the boil. Gently simmer for 15 minutes, until the potatoes are cooked.

Add the croutons and the roast garlic cloves and simmer for a further 5 minutes. Taste for seasoning and adjust if necessary. Pour in the beaten egg, stirring as you go. Serve with chopped parsley on top.

Gruel

This is really 'panada', but I couldn't resist calling it gruel, which is more or less how the late Alan Davidson describes it in his *Oxford Companion to Food* (1999). It is the seventeenth-century equivalent to Heinz Tomato Soup – essential for all invalids. Traditionally it was old bread boiled up with water and, if you were lucky, wine, lemon and sugar.

(Hopefully,) needless to say I've endeavoured to make this version as delicious as possible while nonetheless maintaining the spirit of the original panada. Or gruel. Serve it as a soup and it will improve your day no end. You could equally serve it as a terrific alternative to bread sauce.

SERVES 4

15g/½oz butter
1 small onion, finely chopped
1 garlic clove, minced
50ml/2fl oz oloroso sherry or a dry marsala or madeira
175g/6oz stale sourdough bread, roughly torn
750ml/25fl oz of the very best chicken stock you can get hold of
1 bay leaf
2 sprigs of thyme
A few shakes of Maggi Liquid Seasoning (optional)
2 tbsp double/heavy cream
Salt and freshly ground black pepper

Melt the butter in a large pan and add the onion and garlic. Season with salt and pepper and sweat gently for 20 minutes or so until softened. Add the sherry, bring to the boil, and simmer for a couple of minutes, then stir in the bread and the stock. Return to the boil, add the bay leaf and thyme then simmer for 10 minutes until thickened and very much gruel-like.

Discard the herbs. Add the Maggi, if using, and the cream. Simmer for a further minute or two, then serve.

Hot dog and pickled jalapeño scramble

This has the faint whiff of student food about it but perhaps that's no bad thing. It's a sort of fridge forage version of *huevos revueltos*, somewhere between an omelette and a scramble, and the kind of dish that will demolish any hangover.

SERVES 1–2

2 tbsp olive oil
1 garlic clove, squished with the flat of a knife
A handful of stale bread cubes
2 frankfurter sausages/hot dogs, roughly chopped
3 eggs
2 tbsp roughly chopped pickled jalapeño peppers
Salt and freshly ground black pepper
A handful of parsley, roughly chopped

Heat the oil in a pan and gently fry the garlic over a medium heat for a minute or two, or until lightly browned, then discard the clove. Add the bread and fry until golden on all sides. Add the sausages and continue to cook for a few minutes, stirring occasionally, until heated through. Add the eggs and keep stirring until lightly scrambled. Fold through the jalapeño, season with a little salt and pepper, and finish with some chopped parsley.

Roast chicken and bread salad

This is inspired by the legendary dish from San Francisco's Zuni Café, though I like to roast the chicken on top of the bread – it makes for a ridiculously juicy, chewy, savoury crumb. You will not need or miss potatoes.

SERVES 4

1 chicken, about 1.5kg/3lb 5oz
Olive oil
A big bunch of woody herbs – rosemary, thyme, tarragon
1 garlic bulb, halved
½ lemon
300g/10½oz stale bread – sourdough, focaccia, ciabatta
100ml/3½fl oz white wine
2 tbsp chopped parsley
2 tbsp pine nuts, toasted
2 tbsp raisins
150g/5½oz watercress
Salt

For the dressing
2 tbsp sherry vinegar
8 tbsp olive oil
1 garlic clove, crushed
½ tsp chilli flakes
1 tbsp Dijon mustard

Remove and unwrap the chicken from the fridge at least an hour before cooking.

Preheat the oven to 180°C fan/200°C/400°F/gas mark 6. Rub the chicken all over with salt and olive oil. Put the herbs inside the chicken's cavity, along with the garlic bulb and lemon. Slice the bread if necessary, then lay on a roasting dish and pour over the wine evenly, before placing the chicken on top. Roast for 1 hour. Remove the chicken to a warm plate to rest. Cut the bread into cubes.

For the dressing, whisk together the vinegar, olive oil, garlic, chilli flakes and mustard. Season with a little salt.

Toss together the vinaigrette, bread, parsley, pine nuts, raisins and watercress, then transfer to a serving dish. Carve the chicken and place on top. Eat.

Grilled mackerel with bagnet vert

This isn't a million miles away from how I make salsa verde, but the bread provides added textural interest, as well as more of a savoury flavour profile.

Serve as an accompaniment to grilled meat or fish, or as part of an antipasti (naturally with extra bread for dipping).

SERVES 4

4 fresh mackerel fillets
1 tsp olive oil
Salt

For the bagnet vert
100g/3½oz sourdough, roughly torn
4 tbsp olive oil
2 tbsp sherry vinegar, plus extra if required
50g/1¾oz parsley leaves
1 tbsp capers
1 garlic clove, roughly chopped
Salt and freshly ground black pepper

First make the bagnet vert. Put the bread in a bowl with the olive oil and vinegar and leave to soak for 10 minutes. Transfer to a food processor with the parsley, capers and garlic, and blend until smooth, loosening with a little water if required. Taste for seasoning and adjust with salt, pepper or extra vinegar if you feel it's needed. Your bagnet vert will keep for three days in the fridge.

Rub the mackerel fillets with the olive oil and season with salt. Place, skin-side down, in a cold non-stick frying pan or skillet and set over a medium-high heat. Cook for 3–4 minutes, without touching it, until you can see the fish is almost cooked through. Turn and cook for a further minute. Serve with the bagnet vert.

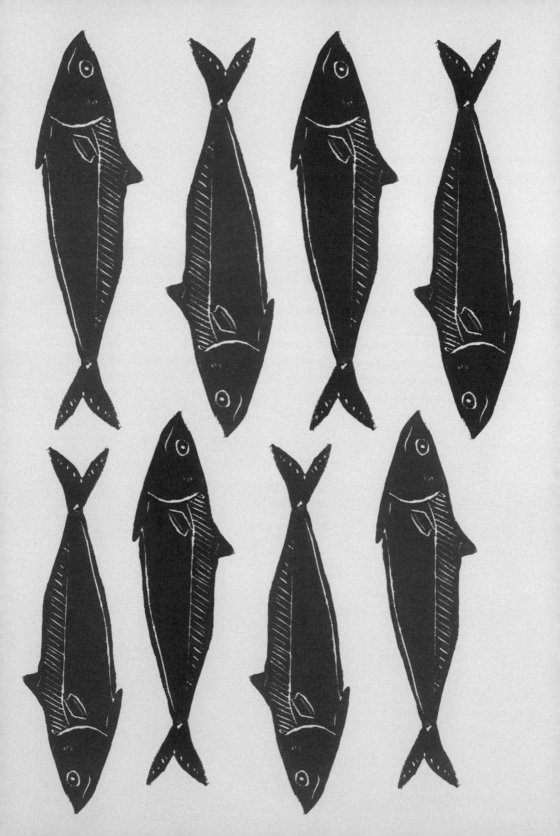

Four savoury bread puddings

BREAD SOUFFLÉ

Whereas a soufflé can be a somewhat stressful dish to produce – it's going to collapse before you get to the table, isn't it? – a bread soufflé is a straightforward and pretty stress-free thing to put together.

SERVES 4–6

25g/1oz softened butter, for greasing
400g/14oz stale bread, torn into chunks
100g/3½oz Parmesan cheese, grated
100g/3½oz mature Cheddar cheese, grated
4 eggs
500ml/18fl oz whole milk
2 tbsp Dijon mustard
A little nutmeg
Salt and freshly ground black pepper

Butter a baking dish, about 30 x 22cm/12 x 9in, or a large soufflé dish.

Arrange half the bread in the bottom of your dish. Scatter over two-thirds of the cheeses, and season with pepper. Put the remaining bread on the top and scatter over the rest of the cheese.

Whisk the eggs, milk, mustard and nutmeg thoroughly. Season with salt and pepper, and pour over the bread. Cover and chill for a minimum of 4 hours, though preferably overnight.

Preheat the oven to 160°C fan/180°C/350°F/gas mark 4. Bake the soufflé for 40–45 minutes, then serve immediately.

SAVOURY BREAD PUDDING

This takes the restrained foundations of the bread soufflé and builds something arguably OTT, but it's a pretty mighty edifice for a dinner. Serve with a green salad and you're away. If you really wanted to juice things up, you could knock up a few Morteau sausages to go alongside.

SERVES 6–8

150g/5½oz softened butter
4 onions, sliced
2 garlic cloves, crushed
1 tsp chopped thyme leaves
125ml/4fl oz red wine
2 tbsp redcurrant jelly (or soft brown sugar)
800g/1lb 12oz stale bread, sliced and cut into triangles
400g/14oz Époisses cheese, sliced (or Brie or Camembert)
5 eggs
650ml/22fl oz whole milk
½ tsp black truffle paste (optional)
Salt and freshly ground black pepper

Melt 50g/1¾oz of the softened butter in a pan over a low heat and very gently fry the onions, along with a pinch of salt, for 45 minutes to 1 hour, stirring occasionally. They should be just turning golden, melting and soft. Stir in the garlic and thyme and cook for a further 5 minutes, then add the wine and redcurrant jelly. Increase the heat to medium-high and simmer until reduced and sticky. Check for seasoning, then leave to cool.

Use a little of the remaining butter to butter a baking dish, about 30 x 22cm/ 12 x 9in, then butter the bread. Arrange a layer of your bread triangles in the bottom of the dish. Top with a third of the cooled onion and a third of the cheese. Repeat, until you have three layers of bread, cheese and onion.

Whisk the eggs with the milk and truffle paste (if using), and season with salt and plenty of pepper. Pour over the dish, cover, and refrigerate for at least 4 hours, ideally overnight.

Preheat the oven to 160°C fan/180°C/350°F/gas mark 4. Bake for 45 minutes or so until golden, bubbling and certain to improve your evening. Eat.

Breakfast strata

Strata is something of a brunch classic in the US, and while I have various issues with the idea of brunch (which I won't go into here), I have absolutely no problem with preparing this a day in advance, so that I can wake up and chuck it in the oven the following morning.

SERVES 6–8

A knob of softened butter, for greasing
700g/1lb 9oz stale bread, sliced
6 eggs
750ml/26fl oz whole milk
350g/12oz cooked Toulouse or other garlicky sausages, thickly sliced
200g/7oz button mushrooms, quartered
350g/12oz cherry tomatoes
200g/7oz Comté or Cheddar cheese, grated
Freshly ground black pepper

Butter a baking dish, about 30 x 22cm/12 x 9in, and press in a layer of the bread slices, using about a third of the bread and tearing up the slices as needed to fill any gaps.

Whisk together the eggs, milk and some black pepper. Scatter half the sausage, mushrooms and tomatoes over the first layer of bread, pour over a third of the custard mix and a good handful of the cheese.

Add another layer of bread, and repeat. Press the final layer of bread on top, and pour over the remaining custard mix. Finish with the last of the cheese, then firmly but gently press down. Wrap in clingfilm/plastic wrap and refrigerate overnight.

In the morning, bake for 45 minutes in a preheated oven at 160°C fan/ 180°C/350°F/gas mark 4, until the custard has set. Have a good breakfast.

Flummadiddle boulangère, sort of

Bread is so integral to how many of us eat day to day that I've been painfully conscious throughout writing this book of marauding around the loaf-eating world appropriating recipes at will. This is absolutely indubitably one of those instances and I can but apologize, but, look, what are you going to do when you come across something called 'Flummadiddle'? Just set it aside and carry on your research?

I'd never heard of it and haven't been able to track down much in the way of recipes, and those that I have found differ wildly. *Wildly*. But Wikipedia describes it as a savoury bread pudding, favoured in particular by New England fishermen, that involves stale bread, pork fat, molasses and spices.

So I figured, why offend one group of people when I could offend two, particularly when that second group is the French! This takes the traditional French practice of baking lamb and potatoes in the residual heat of the village boulanger's oven, but instead does so with pork and bread, to really maximize the pork fat action in play.

Without further ado, but with apology to the New England fishing community and French people, herewith:

SERVES 4

750g/1lb 10oz pork belly off the bone, skin scored
300g/10½oz stale bread, sliced
100g/3½oz pork fat – available in large supermarkets and online
1 tsp ground cinnamon
1 tsp ground allspice
½ tsp ground cloves
2 apples, peeled and thinly sliced
2 onions, thinly sliced
2 tsp finely chopped rosemary needles
500ml/18fl oz pork or chicken stock
Fine sea salt and freshly ground black pepper

Preheat the oven to 150°C fan/170°C/340°F/gas mark 3½. Rub the pork belly all over with a tablespoon of fine sea salt. Spread your slices of stale bread with the pork fat. Arrange a layer of bread in a roasting tray or baking dish that is as close to the size of the pork belly as possible. Mix the spices and toss with the apple, onion and rosemary, and season with salt and pepper. Arrange a handful of the spice mix on top of the bread. Repeat with another layer of bread slices and spice mix, then place the pork belly on top.

Bring the stock to the boil, then pour over the pork skin, filling up the dish to just below the top of the bread. This might seem counter-intuitive for crackling, but it shrinks the skin away from the fat and flesh and, ultimately, helps it to crisp up. Pat the pork dry.

Roast in the oven for 90 minutes. Remove and increase the temperature to 200°C fan/220°C/425°F/gas mark 7. Put the pork belly in a separate roasting pan and return to the oven until the skin is crackling, giving the bread mix, which is your flummadiddle, a 5- to 10-minute blast at the end to get back to temperature and to colour the top of the bread. Carve the pork belly and serve with the flummadiddle and a few of your five a day.

DAY FIVE

Crumbs

Breadcrumbs are a key component of any right-minded cook's
kitchen arsenal. There is something synergistic about the way an ingredient
that would otherwise be borderline useless – stale bread – can enhance
the elements around it, adding crunch to fried food, savouriness
and texture to pasta or risotto, body and depth to sauces and sausages,
and complexity to ice cream.

Recipes tend to ask for dry or fresh (or panko) breadcrumbs.
For the purposes of this chapter it slightly depends on how stale your loaf is
on day five, but assuming it's not brick-like enough to fell a duck,
once you've whizzed up the loaf in a food processor your crumbs shouldn't
be entirely desiccated, and will therefore err on the side of 'fresh'. If the
recipe requires dried breadcrumbs, leave them out for a few hours,
or pop in a low oven for 20 minutes; either method will dry them out.
If I don't say either way then it means it doesn't hugely matter.

As for panko breadcrumbs, these are a quite remarkable invention and I
thoroughly recommend you watch a YouTube video on how they are made.
But they don't really fit in this book because, unless you are baking using
an electrical current, and have the required machinery for grating
the resultant crustless bread to make flakes, you will not have panko
breadcrumbs. Nevertheless, if you're more interested in making great food
than you are in using up an old loaf, panko are pretty peerless for frying.

Old bread and black pudding

This is a great way of using up bread so stale that it's on the verge of becoming a viable weapon. Inspired by the Spanish–Portuguese dish *migas* (meaning 'crumbs'), this has the earthy funk of morcilla or black pudding added. Clears the nostrils.

SERVES 2

150g/5½oz stale bread, cut into small cubes
100ml/3½fl oz milk
2 tbsp olive oil, plus 1 tsp to fry the eggs
1 small onion, roughly chopped
1 small garlic clove, very finely chopped
100g/3½oz morcilla or black pudding, sliced
100g/3½oz spicy cooking chorizo, sliced
1 red pepper, de-seeded and very finely sliced
½ tsp sweet smoked paprika
1 tbsp sherry vinegar
2 eggs
Salt and freshly ground black pepper

Put the bread in a bowl and add the milk. Toss to coat evenly and leave for at least 1 hour, though conceivably overnight.

Heat the 2 tablespoons of olive oil in a large frying pan or skillet. Add the onion and fry gently for 15 minutes, stirring occasionally, until golden and softened. Add the garlic and cook for a further minute, then add the morcilla and chorizo. Turn up the heat and fry for a further 5 minutes or so until crisp here and there. Add the red pepper, paprika and vinegar, cover, turn the heat down to low and cook for 20 minutes until the pepper is soft.

Drain the bread of excess milk, then add to the pan and cook, uncovered, for a further 10 minutes.

Meanwhile, fry the eggs in a separate pan in the teaspoon of olive oil. Season with salt and pepper and serve together with the bread and black pudding.

Jansson's temptation

Simon Hopkinson – the great Simon Hopkinson I think is his official title – insists on using the Abba brand of anchovies for this recipe, though my Swedish friend Em was repulsed when I posted these on Instagram. I can't tell you who knows best but I can tell you that the branding alone makes these worth an investigative purchase. That said, they are certainly unusual and arguably challengingly sweet, and so you may be more comfortable sticking to regular anchovies, which is what Em suggests. And she's Swedish so she must know.

SERVES 8 AS A SIDE, 4 AS A MAIN

1kg/2lb 4oz large waxy potatoes
75g/2¾oz butter
2 onions, thinly sliced
2 x 125g/4½oz cans Abba Grebbestads Ansjovis
   or 80g/3oz (drained weight) anchovy fillets
250ml/9fl oz chicken stock
250ml/9fl oz double/heavy cream
A good handful of dried breadcrumbs
Salt and freshly ground black pepper

Preheat the oven to 170°C fan/190°C/375°F/gas mark 5.

Peel the potatoes and cut into small sticks, about 1cm/½in thick. Rinse under cold water for a couple of minutes, then drain and dry.

Use a little of the butter to grease a baking dish, about 30 x 22cm/12 x 9in, and arrange the onions over the base.

If using the Swedish anchovies, pour the juice of one can over the onions. Roughly chop the anchovies and scatter over the onions, then season with black pepper. Arrange the potatoes on top, then pour over the stock and cream. Season with a little more pepper and a pinch of salt. Finally scatter over the breadcrumbs and then dot with the remaining butter.

Bake for 1 hour. Eat.

Salmorejo

A rogue soup in the wrong place you might think, though while the soups in the previous chapter tend to work with whole hunks of bread, this one seems to work nicely with crumbs. I remember my first encounter with this elixir as if it were last week – a hot day in Jerez perhaps 10 years ago, lunch in the sunshine, buckets of iced fino sherry, and this chilled tomato soup garnished with salted tuna. Killer.

SERVES 4

1kg/2lb 4oz high-grade tomatoes
200g/7oz fresh breadcrumbs
2 garlic cloves, minced
2 tsp sherry vinegar
100ml/3½fl oz olive oil, plus extra for serving
2 medium eggs
A handful of good jamon, roughly torn (optional)
Salt

Purée the tomatoes in a blender, then pass through a sieve. Discard the gunk, then return the tomato purée to your blender with the breadcrumbs, garlic and vinegar. Blend until smooth, then pour in the olive oil as you continue to blend. Season with salt and taste, remembering that when it's served cold (as it will be) the intensity of flavour will be slightly diminished.

Chill for at least 2 hours.

Meanwhile, boil the eggs for 6 minutes then leave to cool before peeling and halving.

Serve the salmorejo with half a boiled egg, ham, if using, and a splash more olive oil.

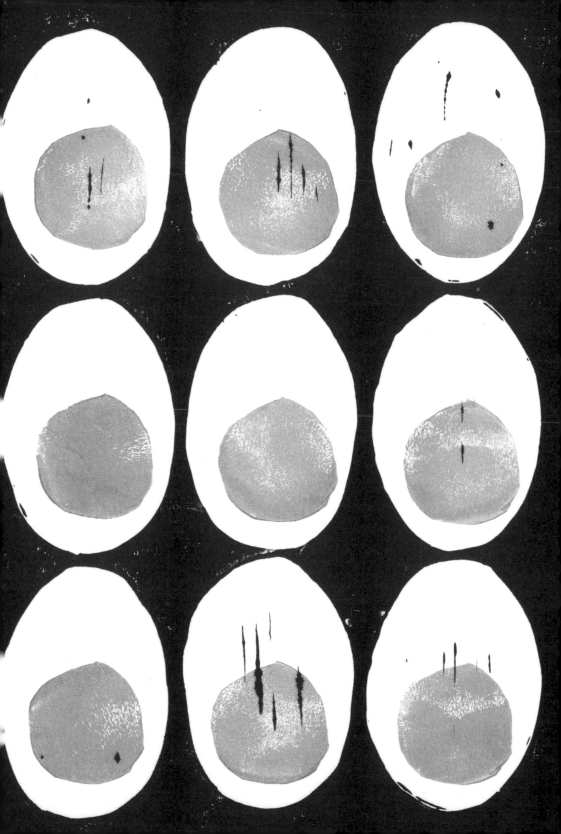

Bread sauce

There's an episode in Bill Buford's highly readable (though now rather problematic due to its subject matter, the rightfully disgraced American chef Mario Batali) book *Heat*, in which celebrity chef Marco Pierre White has something of a tantrum as a result of an over-cloved bread sauce. 'One f*cking clove,' he hisses. 'You're not making a f*cking dessert.' At the other end of the spectrum, Delia Smith goes full Blue Peter on her onion, pincushioning it with cloves until it looks like a hedgehog, or morning star.

All that is to say, it's dealer's choice when it comes to the clove action here. As it is with which bread you use – I quite like a brooding, brown, crusty and savoury bread sauce, though if you prefer something white, then you will need white breadcrumbs. Which you probably figured.

Try the Gruel/panada on page 87 as an alternative sometime.

MAKES ENOUGH FOR 4 TO ENJOY WITH A ROAST CHICKEN

350ml/12fl oz whole milk
½ onion
Between 1 and 1000 cloves, depending on preference
½ tsp white peppercorns
1 bay leaf
75g/2¾oz fresh breadcrumbs
50g/1¾oz butter
Sea salt

Pour the milk into a small saucepan. Stud the onion with your clove(s) and lower into the milk along with the peppercorns and bay leaf. Bring to a gentle simmer, remove from the heat, then leave to infuse for 20 minutes.

Strain the milk into a fresh saucepan, then add the breadcrumbs and bring back to a simmer over a gentle heat. Add the butter and allow to melt. Season with a good pinch of salt and keep warm until ready to serve.

Pangrattato

This is 'grated bread', if you want a literal translation. It's one of those staples that Jamie Oliver seems to bung on everything and, you know, perhaps he's on to something. Particularly with an enhanced version – as I believe this is – having a massively flavourful and textural ingredient that you can add last minute to a salad, a pasta, a risotto, a plate of eggs, even a roast dinner, is the sort of flourish that might just make you feel like a chef.

This pangrattato is amped up with pine nuts, a little smoke, a little spice and a lot of herbs. It will keep in a cool, dry place for a few days.

MAKES 1 JAR

1 tsp coriander seeds
2 tbsp pine nuts
1 tbsp olive oil
1 garlic clove, unpeeled and just lightly crushed
100g/3½oz fresh breadcrumbs
¼ tsp hot smoked paprika
1 tbsp finely chopped parsley
1 tsp finely chopped thyme leaves
¼ tsp dried oregano
Sea salt

Gently toast the coriander seeds in a dry frying pan or skillet until fragrant. Tip into a pestle and mortar, leave to cool, then lightly crush.

In the same pan, toast the pine nuts until golden, then add the olive oil and garlic. Fry for 30 seconds before adding the breadcrumbs, smoked paprika and your crushed coriander. Continue to fry over a medium heat, stirring almost constantly, until the breadcrumbs are crispy and golden brown. Toss through the herbs, remove from the heat, and season with sea salt.

Glamorgan sausages

You could call this a cheese and leek croquette but I quite like how the name here – and I hope this doesn't offend people from Glamorgan – underpromises and overdelivers.

MAKES 12 SAUSAGES

25g/1oz butter
1 large leek, trimmed and finely chopped
1 tsp chopped thyme leaves
200g/7oz grated Caerphilly cheese (or mature Cheddar)
300g/10½oz fine breadcrumbs
3 eggs
5 tbsp whole milk
1 tbsp Dijon mustard
2 tbsp finely chopped parsley
125g/4½oz plain/all-purpose flour
200ml/7fl oz vegetable oil
Salt and freshly ground black pepper

Melt the butter over a gentle heat in a large pan and sweat the leeks along with the thyme and a little salt and pepper for 20–25 minutes, until softened. Transfer to a mixing bowl and add the cheese, two-thirds of the breadcrumbs, two of the eggs, the milk, mustard and parsley and mix thoroughly. Taste for seasoning and adjust if necessary. Divide into 12 pieces, roll into sausages, then cover and chill for at least an hour – the longer you chill, the easier the next step with be.

On three separate plates, line up the flour, the last egg (beaten), and the rest of your breadcrumbs. Season the flour with a little salt. Roll the sausages first in the flour (jiggling off any excess), then the egg and finally the breadcrumbs. Cover and chill again for 15 minutes or so.

Heat the oil in a heavy-bottomed sauté pan to 180°C/350°F (a piece of bread should fizzle on impact). Fry the sausages for 2–3 minutes on each side until golden. Remove to drain on kitchen paper, then eat as soon as possible.

Braised pig cheeks with tomato and almond salsa

A good do-ahead dinner that packs a punch. The sauce is somewhere in the vicinity of a romesco but I don't want to start a fight with any Catalonians by claiming anything close to authenticity here. Serve with a few potatoes and a green salad.

SERVES 4

For the pig cheeks
1 tsp olive oil
12 pig cheeks, trimmed of any excess fat or gristle
1 onion, finely chopped
2 garlic cloves, sliced
150ml/5fl oz dry oloroso sherry or red wine
300ml/10fl oz dark chicken or pork stock
2 sprigs of rosemary
1 tbsp tomato purée/paste
Salt and freshly ground black pepper

For the sauce
250g/9oz ripe tomatoes or two large, ripe tomatoes
2 tbsp olive oil
50g/1¾oz toasted almonds
50g/1¾oz breadcrumbs
1 garlic clove, minced
125g/4½oz roasted red peppers (from a jar)
1 tbsp sherry vinegar
½ tsp chilli flakes

Heat the olive oil in a sauté pan and, working in batches so as not to overcrowd the pan, brown the pig cheeks all over, seasoning with salt and pepper as you do. Set aside on a separate plate. Reduce the heat and gently fry the onion and garlic for about 20 minutes until soft. Return the cheeks to the pan, jack up the heat, and add the sherry or wine. Simmer for 1 minute or so, then add the stock, rosemary and tomato purée. Bring back to a gentle simmer, cover and simmer for 1½ hours until the cheeks are tender.

Meanwhile, make the sauce. Halve the tomatoes and toss with the olive oil. Put under a hot grill/broiler for 15-20 minutes and cook until lightly coloured and softened. Blitz in a food processor with the almonds, breadcrumbs, garlic, peppers, vinegar and chilli flakes. Season with salt and taste. Add a little more salt – or vinegar – if necessary.

Remove the pig cheeks from the pan and keep warm. Pass the cooking liquor through a fine sieve into a clean pan and simmer to reduce until sticky.

Serve the cheeks with the salsa and some of the jus spooned over.

Meatloaf

As the child of an American mother I was treated to meatloaf on a semi-regular basis when growing up. This recipe comes from one of my grandmother Dee Dee's recipe books – the *Pacific ls Pantry*, by the Women's Guild of Omaha, Nebraska for the Pacific Hills Lutheran Church (1959). I dare say it's out of print.

SERVES 8

200g/7oz fresh breadcrumbs
225ml/7¾fl oz whole milk
750g/1lb 10oz minced/ground beef – not too lean
2 eggs, lightly beaten
1 onion, grated
2 tbsp finely chopped sage
2 tbsp brown sugar
50g/1¾oz ketchup
1 tsp mustard powder
A little grated nutmeg
Salt and freshly ground black pepper

Preheat the oven to 160°C fan/180°C/350°F/gas mark 4.

Soak the breadcrumbs in the milk for 10 minutes, then add the beef, eggs, onion and sage, and season with salt and pepper. Mix well, then transfer into a greased loaf tin.

Mix the sugar, ketchup, mustard powder and nutmeg and spoon over the top of the loaf.

Bake for 45 minutes. Rest for 15 minutes. Slice and serve or, even better, wait until tomorrow and eat cold in a sandwich.

Veal Holstein

There are several details here which are key to the success of this dish, and which is why this serves two people. Any more and you'll lose focus – or I certainly would – overcrowd the pan, and just quietly drop it from a 10/10 to an 8/10, and no one wants that. If you're feeling brave, bold, or have an absolutely enormous frying pan or skillet, by all means double the recipe.

SERVES 2

2 rose veal escalopes (or pork, if you prefer) – around 150g/5½oz each
2 tbsp plain/all-purpose flour
1 egg, beaten, for coating
75g/2¾oz fresh breadcrumbs
3 tbsp groundnut or other neutral oil
2 eggs
30g/1oz butter
1 tsp capers (preferably the small non-pareil kind)
1 tbsp chopped parsley
½ lemon
6 anchovy fillets
Salt and freshly ground black pepper

Lightly flatten the escalopes with a rolling pin until they're of even thickness. Season with salt and pepper. On three separate plates, line up the flour, the egg and the breadcrumbs. Lightly dust the escalopes first in the flour, then in the egg, and finally coat thoroughly in the breadcrumbs.

Heat 2 tablespoons of the oil in a large frying pan or skillet, and fry the escalopes for 3–4 minutes on each side until golden. Remove and keep warm. Add the remaining oil to the pan and fry the eggs gently.

Meanwhile, melt the butter in a small saucepan over a medium heat until it starts to brown, then add the capers, parsley and a squeeze of lemon juice.

Serve the escalopes with a fried egg, a few anchovy fillets, and the caper sauce.

Chorizo dumplings

I wondered if there was a way to knock up some quick dumplings using bread, as opposed to making a dough from scratch, and sure enough there is, one that the Germans call semmelknödel. This is a very vague approximation of those, which I think would make a knock-out dumpling baked into a stew, though otherwise serve alongside one, or with soup. Or just, you know, eat them.

MAKES 8 DUMPLINGS

A splash of olive oil
150g/5½oz spicy cooking chorizo, finely diced
300g/10½oz dried breadcrumbs, plus extra just in case
150ml/5fl oz whole milk
2 eggs, lightly beaten
4 spring onions/scallions, finely chopped
4 tbsp parsley, finely chopped
Salt and freshly ground black pepper

Heat a little olive oil in a sauté pan or skillet and fry the chorizo until lightly crisped and the oil is a rusty puddle. Remove with a slotted spoon, reserving the oil.

Soak the breadcrumbs in the milk for 10 minutes, then squeeze out excess moisture. Transfer to a clean bowl, then add the fried chorizo, chorizo oil, eggs, spring onion and parsley, season with salt and pepper and bring together with a metal spoon. The mixture should be dense and somewhat claggy. If a little loose, add more breadcrumbs.

Form into balls and chill for 30 minutes.

Bring a pan of salted water to a gentle simmer and lower in the dumplings. Simmer for 15–20 minutes. Serve.

Cassoulet

Cassoulet makes double use of breadcrumbs by baking a layer of breadcrumbs on top, then stirring that layer through the pot halfway through cooking as a thickener, and replacing it with a fresh layer of crumbs for the final crunch.

This is a bit of a project dish but requires little technical brilliance and is a wonderful thing to bring to the table with a flourish.

SERVES 6–8

600g/1lb 5oz dried haricot beans, soaked overnight
   (or 2 x 400g/14oz canned beans)
1 head of garlic, halved horizontally
2 bay leaves
A bunch of thyme
1 lamb shank, or ham hock
2 confit duck legs (shop-bought)
500g/1lb 2oz pork belly, sliced
3 Toulouse sausages
1 onion, very finely chopped
4 garlic cloves, minced
2 tbsp tomato purée/paste
200g/7oz breadcrumbs
2 tbsp sage, very finely chopped
Freshly ground black pepper

I'll be honest – I rarely bother to buy dried beans, so skip this first step if you prefer and add canned beans to the onions in step 3 below, but you will have to have cooked the lamb shank before you move on, or forfeit it altogether. So – take your soaked beans and put them in a deep pan of water along with the garlic, bay leaves, thyme and lamb shank. Bring to the boil and simmer gently for 1½–2 hours, until the beans are tender and the lamb is falling off the bone. Remove the lamb shank, cool, then strip off the meat and discard the bone. Drain the beans, reserving the cooking liquor.

Preheat the oven to 130°C fan/150°C/300°F/gas mark 2. Scoop a couple of tablespoons of the fat from the confit duck into your most handsome cast-iron casserole, and get it nice and hot on the hob. Brown the confit duck legs all over, then pop them in the warm oven for now. Brown the pork belly on both sides, and remove to a plate, then repeat with the sausages. Fry the onion gently in the residual fat until totally softened. Probably 20 minutes, maybe 30. Meanwhile strip the meat from the duck legs.

Right, nearly there. Stir the garlic and tomato purée into the onions, then add the beans, lamb, duck, pork belly and sausages. Stir to combine. Mix the breadcrumbs and sage and scatter half over the top. Cook for 1 hour. Remove, and stir the breadcrumbs through, then scatter the remaining breadcrumbs over the top. Cook for a further hour. Season with black pepper and salt, to taste. Eat.

Sticky citrus cake

I've lost count of how many times I've made this in some form or other over the years. It was part of the course I took at Ballymaloe Cookery School in Cork in the Republic of Ireland, and very much part of the menus served at my supper club in north London. People go nuts for it, and it's about as easy a cake as you'll ever make. If you wanted to make it gluten free (which would be weird, given you're reading this book) you could sub out the breadcrumbs for polenta.

FOR A 20-CM/8-IN CAKE

50g/1¾oz breadcrumbs
100g/3½oz ground almonds
200g/7oz caster/superfine sugar
1½ tsp baking powder
200ml/7fl oz olive oil, plus extra for greasing
4 eggs, lightly beaten
Zest of 1 orange
Zest of 1 lemon
Sea salt

For the syrup
Juice of the orange and lemon (used for the cake), weighed
Equal weight of caster/superfine sugar
4 cardamom pods
1 cinnamon stick

To finish
Toasted almond flakes
Crème fraîche

Grease a 20-cm/8-in cake tin with a little oil, and line the base with baking/parchment paper.

Place a non-stick frying pan or skillet over a moderate heat and toast the breadcrumbs and ground almonds until golden and fragrant. Decant into a mixing bowl, then stir in the sugar, baking powder, olive oil, eggs, orange and lemon zest and a small pinch of sea salt. Combine thoroughly but don't overwork.

Transfer the mixture to your prepared cake tin and introduce to a cold oven. Turn the oven on and heat to 150°C fan/170°C/340°F/gas mark 3½. Bake for 50–60 minutes (timed from when you switched the oven on) until golden on top and a skewer inserted into the centre comes out clean.

Meanwhile, in a small saucepan, whisk together the juice and sugar and bring to a gentle boil with the cardamom and cinnamon. Simmer for 3 minutes then leave to cool.

Remove the baked cake from the oven and leave in the tin for 10 minutes in a cool place. Carefully turn out onto a handsome plate. Prick it all over with a skewer, then pour over the syrup.

Finish with toasted almond flakes and serve warm or cold with some crème fraîche.

Bread ice cream with salted maple and rosemary breadcrumbs

You can play around with what bread you use here, but I find it hard to beat the nutty, malty characteristics you get from good brown bread. We used to have this all the time as kids, which is odd considering it now seems rather a modern and, dare I say, trendy kind of ice cream – perhaps there are no new ideas left after all.

There shouldn't be any need to churn this ice cream.

SERVES 6

For the ice cream
100g/3½oz fresh brown breadcrumbs
600ml/20fl oz double/heavy cream
1 vanilla pod
100g/3½oz soft dark brown sugar
4 egg yolks
A pinch of grated nutmeg or cinnamon
A pinch of sea salt

For the breadcrumbs
1 tbsp olive oil
1 sprig of rosemary
50g/1¾oz breadcrumbs
3 tbsp maple syrup
Sea salt

Begin by making the ice cream. Toast the breadcrumbs in a dry non-stick frying pan or skillet, then set aside.

Pour the cream into a saucepan and add the vanilla pod. Set over a low heat and very slowly bring the cream to the boil. Meanwhile, in a heavy bottomed mixing bowl, whisk together the sugar and egg yolks until pale and light. When the cream is at the boil, pour it straight onto the egg yolks while whisking continuously. Fold in the breadcrumbs, a little nutmeg or cinnamon and a pinch of sea salt, then leave to cool before freezing in a freezerproof container.

To make the salted maple rosemary breadcrumbs, heat the olive oil in a non-stick frying pan or skillet and gently fry the rosemary for 1 minute, before adding the breadcrumbs. Continue to fry over a medium-high heat, stirring regularly, until starting to crisp up. Add the maple syrup and a pinch of sea salt and let it simmer gently for another minute or two, then discard the rosemary and leave the breadcrumbs to cool.

Eat the ice cream topped with the breadcrumbs.

Treacle tart

This recipe first appeared in my second book, *Do-Ahead Dinners*. By all means use shop-bought shortcrust pastry.

SERVES 6–8

For the pastry
100g/3½oz cold butter, cubed
200g/7oz plain/all-purpose flour
½ tsp salt
2 eggs

For the filling
450g/1lb golden syrup/dark corn syrup
100g/3½oz breadcrumbs
Zest of 1 lemon
1 egg, lightly beaten
1 tsp sea salt

To make the pastry, rub the butter into the flour until it resembles breadcrumbs, then add the salt and one of the eggs and mix to form a dough. If it's too dry add a little splash of cold water. Wrap in clingfilm/plastic wrap and chill in the freezer for 10 minutes.

Now roll out the dough on a lightly floured surface and line a 20-cm/8-in tart tin. Pop this back in the freezer. Preheat the oven to 150°C fan/170°C/340°F/gas mark 3½.

Line the tart case/shell with baking/parchment paper and tip in something to weigh it down – baking beans, dried chickpeas, the contents of your piggy bank – then bake for 25 minutes. Remove from the oven and tip out the baking beans. Beat the second egg and brush it over the pastry, then bake for a further 10 minutes. Remove from the oven and lower the temperature to 120°C fan/140°C/275°F/gas mark 1.

Mix together the filling ingredients and tip into the tart case. Bake for 50–60 minutes until set. Serve warm or cold.

Kvass

Kvass is, essentially, a fermented bread beer and will knock your socks off. I came across it during a relatively brief and not altogether successful stint teaching in Moscow. It was a stinking hot June day and in that moment – as is so often the case when appetite and weather and mood align – it seemed like the most delicious thing I'd ever tasted.

This is also a good way of using up discarded sourdough starter if you have any kicking about. Your kvass will last for a couple of weeks in the fridge. Check the CO_2 levels every now and then to avoid an explosion.

MAKES ABOUT 4 LITRES/4 QUARTS

500g/1lb 2oz sourdough or rye bread, sliced
100g/3½oz raisins
100g/3½oz grapes
Peeled rind of 1 lemon
350g/12oz liquid molasses
1 tbsp active dry yeast, or 4 tbsp discarded sourdough starter and a pinch of active yeast

You'll also need
4 x 1 litre/1 quart soda bottles or swing-top kilner bottles, sterilized

Bring 5 litres/5 quarts water to the boil in a large pan. Meanwhile toast the bread *hard*. It needs to be on the verge of burning (without actually burning). Add the toast, raisins, grapes and lemon rind to the water, take off the heat, and leave to soak overnight.

Remove the bread a slice at a time, pressing the excess liquid back into the pot. Whisk in the molasses and yeast thoroughly, then cover and leave for a further 6 hours, whisking every now and then.

Remove the raisins, grapes and lemon rind. Strain the liquid through a muslin/cheesecloth into a clean pan or bowl, then carefully decant into the sterilized bottles. Stopper the bottles, but leave them open enough for air to escape. Leave in a cool dry place for a day or two, tasting occasionally. Once slightly sour and fizzy, stopper fully and refrigerate. Serve very cold.

Index

Acknowledgements

I'm incredibly grateful to everyone at Pavilion for their enthusiasm, insight and good humour in getting this book from idle lockdown daydream to actual paper and ink; in particular to my editor Cara Armstrong and designer Nicky Collings, and to 'head girl' Polly Powell for her continued support.

Thank you also to Ellie Edwards for your subtle and stylish illustrations - they bring everything into life and focus in such a witty, understated way.

I'm very lucky to have a friend first, and agent second in Claudia Young, who I've known since the early days of supper clubs over a decade ago, and who is one of the more brilliant and silly people to spend a long and badly behaved afternoon with; and thank you to Holly Faulks for shepherding this book through some key stages of its inception while Claudia was on maternity leave.

A big thanks to Stephanie Evans for such forensic and astute copy-editing. I'm not one to make excuses but writing a book while trying to homeschool two unruly children led to more than a few syntactical, grammatical and other recipe-based howlers and you appear to have spotted them all.

Particular thanks to Sam Herlihy. He asked me to say that. But I do love him.

Other people to whom I owe thanks include but are not limited to Will Palmer, Ian Campbell, Feri Nemcsik, Felicity Cloake, and the truly wonderful and world-class gangs at Pidgin, Sons + Daughters, the 10 Cases, and Drop.

And to Rosie, Thom-Thom and Nora, I give thanks every day for being the best family imaginable. You even ate the gruel. I love you more than words can possibly express.